nake the biggest difference. **The smallest change** can make the biggest differen
difference. The smallest change **can make the** biggest difference. The smallest
nallest change can make the **biggest difference.** The smallest change can make

Dedicated to the two loves of my life
Em & Hannah

*"Consider for a moment, a car that is travelling in a straight line from Nashville, Tennessee to Los Angeles, California. If you moved the steering wheel just one quarter of an inch to the right, the car would probably end up in Vancouver, British Columbia.*

*The smallest change or improvement in your ATTITUDE will dramatically affect where you will be five years from now, ten years from now, and so on. Over the period of a lifetime, it would be difficult to even guess at how a small improvement in your ATTITUDE, will improve every aspect of your life."*

Bob Proctor
- The Goal Achiever Program

Copyright © 2012 by Stuart Young

This edition first published 2012.

ISBN:          Softcover              978-1-4691-8132-5
               Ebook                  978-1-4691-8133-2

Cover Design by: Stuart Young
Cover Photography by: Hannah Young

–   (www.flickr.com/photos/hyoungphotography)

Internal layout by: Stuart Young
Contact Stuart direct at: stuart.young40@googlemail.com

This book was printed in the United States of America.

**To order additional copies of this book, contact:**
Xlibris Corporation
0-800-644-6988
www.xlibrispublishing.co.uk
Orders@xlibrispublishing.co.uk
303752

# Contents

# What is this book about and why did I write it?

We all want to change our lives for the better in some way shape or form, me included. If however you're prone to saying things like: 'My life would be better if my boss this or that' or 'My life would be better if my mother this or that' or 'My life would be better if my friends this or that' or 'My life would be better if the government this or that' - then let me tell you something - nothing is going to change in your life for the better whilst you continue to blame others for *your* circumstances. I'm not saying that they didn't have a hand in your circumstances, I'm saying only YOU can decide to change your circumstances for the better. STOP complaining and start *being* different so you can *do* things differently.

I've read books and taken coaching programs and experienced hypnotherapy and NLP therapy in the past - all of which have helped me figure out how to change things about myself which in turn have helped change my circumstances. Have they taken a lot of time and effort - yes! Did it take a process of continual searching (which is still ongoing) to find these influences - yes! Will this book act as a substitute for all that - possibly, but probably not. But what it will do is get you moving in the right direction from day one. Think of this book as complimentary to any and every other self improvement course or therapy available. As you continue on your own journey of self improvement allow the guides in this book to perpetually encourage you forwards. You may look back in the future and decide that something written here was the turning point.

This book started off as a series of Tweets - *"Take the opportunity today to hug someone you love, just for the hell of it! :)"*. That was the first one, then out came another and another and pretty soon I was thinking of them every day. As the days ticked on I found myself thinking of more and more opportunities, each one having the possibility to change my life on that day, sometimes in a small way, sometimes in a big way. Eventually I decided to do one a day for an entire year and document my experiences in a journal.

This book is, in part, that journal. Each day that passed I tried to apply one thing, one opportunity to make a difference. Sometimes just to myself, and other times to those around me. Sometimes to complete strangers. I then documented how that affected me, how it changed me, my attitudes, my beliefs, fears, anxieties and so on. Each day that I successfully completed a task I wrote down how I actually applied the 'guide', then how it made me feel and in some cases what actually happened because of it.

It's tempting from time to time to think we need to make a big change in our lives, we can feel it building up as we resist it with our inaction. But maybe the biggest change can come about as a result of the accumulation of lots of little changes.

*"The truth be told, success typically follows a series of little events and achievements that can seem to take an eternity, that include a few disappointments along the way, and that challenge everything about you to the core - your stamina, courage, integrity, and even your willingness to keep going."* - Jack Canfield

Don't get the idea that I think that I now have the perfect life - I don't, nobody does, it's a work in progress. And that's the key word 'progress', if you're not making progress, if you're not improving your life piece by piece - you'll stagnate. If it's because you're not sure how, then apply these guides and I promise they WILL make a difference and that difference will be an *improvement* in some way shape or form.

Let me be clear right at the start though - I am not a doctor, I am not a psychiatrist, I am not a therapist or a life coach. I'm just a normal, everyday person like you. So if I can make a change in my life without studying some complicated therapeutic system or going through a lengthy self analysis process, then so can you. This book is simply a set of practical ideas - easy to implement (although some will take a lot of courage or tenacity), and repeatable over and over again.

By applying these guides you will feel more in control. Control of your actions; as you decide which guides to try, more control of your emotions; as you'll feel a certain way before deciding to act, and ultimately more control of your life; as you begin to see the consequences of those actions.

I have met many people that moan about the world at large, about the government, about the local council and when I suggest they do something about it they say: "What can I do? I'm only one person." This portrays the feeling of helplessness. Of a lack of control of our environment or circumstances. These feelings of being helpless can lead to feelings of depression, unhappiness, low self esteem, a lack of confidence and inadequacy. By taking control of our lives, even in small ways at first, we can potentially reverse the fall towards those negative feelings. By stepping outside of our comfort zone we give ourselves the opportunity to see that we make a difference. Once we see that on the small scale we tend to start seeing it on a larger and larger scale. I urge you now to take more control of your life.

Chaos theory, otherwise known as the Butterfly Effect suggests that the tiniest of changes can have dramatic repercussions, so don't try and second guess what effect your actions will have, you'll notice it as it happens.

I hope that you will decide to apply these guides to your own life and see how it affects you and possibly those around you. Keep a journal of your experiences and I guarantee that at some point during the year you WILL notice changes happening in your life. Try to resist the urge to skip ahead and do more than one a day, in my experience the biggest changes happened when I tried to apply just one idea throughout the whole day. And if I managed to complete it really easily then I spent the rest of the day pondering it and how it made me feel. This is an important part of the process so please, don't rush ahead. Instead take each day as it comes - a bit like life really. :) I would even go as far as to suggest that you resist even looking ahead to what challenges are coming and just surrender to them as you find them each day - afresh!

(Tip: I used a standard little diary to record each challenge - I just made a quick note about what I did and how it made me feel, this way if I missed doing a challenge on a particular day I could easily go back through my diary, find it, and do it on another day that perhaps, I had completed that day's task already. My own diary entries are those bits in the grey boxes at the foot of the pages, and they weren't all done on the actual day believe me.)

Use this little book each day to help you make the small changes in your life that could eventually become a major shift in your life experience. The number one quickest sure fire way to experience something is to enable someone else to experience it (Neale Donald

Walsch said something like that!). And he was right! That's why many of the daily guides are about doing things for other people. Some are simple and will only take 5 minutes, others will require some deep thought, others courage and determination. There's no telling which will make the biggest impact, so try them all - you will be pleasantly surprised. Go out of your way, make the effort and you will feel happier, more fulfilled, more powerful and more love in your life. I urge you, before you start, do them in order. The first initial few are designed to ease you in to a frame of mind of love, compassion, service and forgiveness. From there you'll find many of the others will be easier to take on. Rush ahead and you might find the emotional resources you need to carry out some of the opportunities are not readily available.

Take the time to think about each guide throughout that particular day and you will find that the opportunity will reveal itself. Take this book with you bookmarked on the day and refer to it constantly - this will remind you to keep looking for the opportunity to reveal itself. Otherwise you go out in the morning with the best intentions, the day starts to get hectic and before you know it you come home without having thought about it once - and the day is gone!

At one point I thought about 'choosing' an opportunity from the list each day but decided that if one day I was feeling particularly lazy I'd choose an easy one. Sounds like a good idea at first doesn't it? Trouble is, I realised that if I chose them on the day, I wouldn't give myself the opportunity to be challenged that day. Imagine I wake up a bit cranky, it happens to us all right? and I go to the list and find that that day's task is to dig deep and find forgiveness for someone, I might find that reeeeaaally hard. But that's the challenge. We can all forgive people if we're in a good mood - the challenge and opportunity to grow lies in finding that forgiveness when we're feeling like a bear with a sore head. So I arranged the opportunities in a semi random way - some simple ones then some hard ones, some to do with others followed by some to do with myself and so on.

I hope you can find the strength to follow them in sequence for no other reason than doing things we don't want to do, when we don't want to do them can actually be the catalyst for the greatest change in our life. But don't get stressed if you really can't find the time to complete a task on the day - this is supposed to *help* you not hinder you. At the end of each month you'll be prompted to look back through the month and revisit any you may have missed.

Before you start, this short exercise might help too - write a list of things you are happy with about your life right now. Then write a list of things you would like to change. It might be something about your circumstances, it might be something about yourself. This will give you a clearer idea of what your life '*could*' look like. Obviously, at this stage you won't know what will change but these lists will give you an insight and help you identify changes as they happen.
At the end of this journey we'll make these lists again and compare them with the first, I don't know about you but I get excited just thinking about that day.

At the end of each month you'll be given the opportunity to make a note of any changes you might have experienced over the previous 30 days. Incrementally your attitude, habits, relationships and life experience will alter. At first it might be difficult to notice but as you become accustomed to looking a little closer you *will* notice them.

> **" Success is the sum of small efforts, repeated day in and day out. "** - Robert Collier

So without further ado I invite you to...Take the opportunity to flip the page over and take the first step towards improving your life.

(PS: If you come to this book later than Jan 1st please just start on the day you start reading and follow it through all the way through the New Year and back to where you started - it doesn't matter so much when you take the opportunities, but that you actually decide to take them. Maybe find the next nearest '*easy*' challenges/guides and start there as I recommend starting with easy ones first to get into the swing of it. Having said that, if you want to start at the very beginning that's ok too! The important thing is to enjoy the process even when it gets a bit tougher.)

# These are some things I'm happy with about my life:
(List at least 10)

_____

_____

_____

_____

_____

_____

_____

_____

_____

_____

_____

_____

# These are some changes I'd like to see in my life:
(List at least 10)

_____

_____

_____

_____

_____

_____

_____

_____

_____

_____

_____

_____

_____

JANUARY 1st
# Take the opportunity today to write down your lifestyle goals.

And by that I mean some goals that will give you more time with your family or more time to enjoy your hobbies. Or maybe you've always wanted to play an instrument or learn a new skill. Maybe it's to achieve something particular or even just to find ways to give back to the community.

Writing them down will make them more real plus the very act of making a list will help you think of things you would like to do, have or achieve. Once you've made a list, organise it into order - it can be a priority order but make sure you put some of the easiest things near or even at the top. This way you will be able to start realising your goals quickly which will spur you on and motivate you to continue the process when you get to the tougher ones.

When I arranged my list on a lined pad, I wrote one goal per page, then underneath that I made some notes about what my first step towards that goal would be. Then I wrote the second step, then third and so on right up to the point where the goal would be achieved. It took me a while but it was worth it as I could see reasonably clearly 'how' I was going to achieve the goal and how I'd recognise I was on track. (This is not set in concrete - allow yourself to be flexible.)

Don't be put off by this time intensive first exercise - what better day is there to make a list of goals than New Year's Day? I say goals rather than resolutions as in my experience if you make a resolution and then a month later you break it, you feel like you have failed. You resolve to give up smoking (that's a common one right?), then on Jan 27th you have a cigarette at a dinner party with friends that are all smoking. The next day you say to yourself 'Oh well, that didn't work', and guess what? you start smoking again. With a goal however, if you decide to smoke less for instance and you manage to go without a cigarrete for over 3 weeks when you usually smoke 30 or 40 a day, you can pat yourself proudly on the back, say to yourself 'Whoh, I went 3 weeks without smoking - now I'm gonna try to go 4 weeks.' You see, you can actually use it as a measure of success which can motivate you to do even better.

I promise over the next few days the guides will be really simple and a lot of fun. :)

JANUARY 2nd

# Take the opportunity today to hug someone you love - just for the hell of it!

As I write this I'm waiting for my other half to come back from walking one of our dogs. When she arrives I'm going to give her a big hug. She won't be surprised as I often hug her for no other reason than it feels good. I do the same with my grown up daughter when I see her too. Hug more. Hug spontaneously. It will make you feel good and it'll make the person you're hugging feel loved and appreciated too.

I lost my mum some years ago and as I think about her right now I think the thing I miss most are the hugs. My mum gave the loveliest bear hugs every time any of us kids saw her - and the grandchildren too. If you're not a touchy feely kind of person you might find this more difficult than I do but try anyway - you'll be glad you did, especially if you can make a habit of it. :)

> **" We have to be the change we want to see in the world. "**
>
> - Gandhi

Hugged my other half when she got in, and again a bit later when we had a cuppa at lunchtime, then again when I just walked in to her office while she was on the phone and gently put my arms around her for a moment. Just consciously thinking about today's task is making me want to hug her more - all day. :)

JANUARY 3rd
# Take the opportunity today to thank someone unexpectedly! It'll change their day. :)

We all like to be thanked, it shows us that we are appreciated and valued and probably more fundamentally - noticed!

As we thank another we are sending that person something intangible and immeasurable. But watch the reaction of the recipient. Some will smile broadly and some will beam proudly while others will have a more subtle reaction. A reaction there will be though. In sending out that thanks you will automatically open yourself to receive it more readily yourself and therefore feel valued and appreciated aswell.

Get in to the habit of enjoying thanking people and it could turn out to be one of the easiest ways to positively influence your life and the lives of those around you. When you search for the opportunity to thank unexpectedly it will have the biggest impact. It's second nature to most people to thank someone if we have the door held open for us or if someone gives us a lift but find that occurrence when someone does something they don't expect you to notice. Maybe the postman will pick up a piece of litter off your front lawn or the shop assistant might run to fetch that bottle of milk you forgot while you're at the checkout. Search for it and you'll find it and when you do you'll find yourself searching for that opportunity all the time.

Have fun looking. :)

JANUARY 4th

# Take the opportunity today to just daydream a little. You'll be glad you did. :)

Some people call it meditation, some call it being still, I call it day-dreaming. When you take the time to do nothing your mind can wander. It can happen while you're doing something mundane, that doesn't need your full attention - washing the car for instance. It can happen while you walk in the woods or the park, as one foot falls in front of the other you find your mind drifting to past events or future dreams.

This is a creative process. One of my goals for the coming year is to spend 15 minutes a day just daydreaming. The idea for this book came from sitting in my kitchen with a cup of tea and one of our dogs at my feet. My other half was out walking our other dog, there was no radio or TV on - it was silent and my mind just drifted.

Try it, it might not bring any fruit the first time but that doesn't matter. The very process of daydreaming is reward enough.

Happy dreaming! :)

Every tuesday I visit a Krishna Temple and buy some carob fudge cake called 'Maha'. Some for me and my other half and some for a pal and his wife where I go drumming - we have it over a cuppa before we play. I decided to sit in the car outside the little Krishna shop and daydream. After a few minutes of thinking of this and that I had the idea for the introduction of this book and how readers might get the best out of it. All in all, a productive 15 minutes. :)

JANUARY 5th
# Take the opportunity today to smile for no real reason. :)

Smiling literally changes the chemical balance in your brain and kick starts the 'happy hormones' in to production. These endorphins actually make you feel better so the simple act of smiling actually makes you *want* to smile. Not to mention the fact that smiling is infectious so make someone else smile today by smiling *at* them. As Louis Armstrong famously said: *"When you're smiling the whole world smiles with you."* Now I don't suppose for a minute he meant that literally but the point is when You are smiling it *feels* like the whole world is smiling along.

Here are a few more famous quotes about the power of smiling:

*"The shortest distance between two people is a smile."* Unknown

*"Smile, it's the second best thing you can do with your lips."* Ian Segail

*"If you see a friend without a smile, give him one of yours."* Proverb

I tried this immediately after writing it down, but I have to say I think it might take practise because it felt a bit awkward. So what I found myself doing was thinking of things to smile about - a memory, a joke, a funny sketch on a TV show - anything! I found myself smiling throughout the day after that. :)

JANUARY 6th

# Take the opportunity today to encourage someone.

This is purely an altruistic challenge, however, by encouraging someone you will find that you actually encourage yourself. If the person you are trying to encourage starts to put a barrier between themselves and what they are trying to achieve, you will find yourself creating solutions to help encourage them forward. By doing so, the next time you yourself feel unable to find a way to achieve something you will automatically employ the same tactic and thereby encourage yourself in the process.

I did this today. I was reading a book called Moondance by Karen M. Black - it was a free download from her website at the time. I emailed her to let her know how much I was enjoying the book and that I thought she had a captivating writing style.

Lo and behold she emailed me back within about an hour expressing thanks that I'd taken the time to write to her with words of encouragement and that she actually thought my abstract art was 'beautiful'. She then asked if she might use some of my images on her websites and newsletters.

As the saying goes: 'What goes around comes around.' :)

# Take the opportunity today to compliment someone. It'll make their day.

You know how it *feels* when somebody tells you how nice you look or what a good piece of work you've just completed or what a kind person you are etc. But are you always aware of how you feel when you compliment someone else?

Be aware the next time you compliment someone and I'm sure you'll find it makes *you* feel good too. So today, make someone's day by complimenting them for something and remember to note how it makes you feel too - I guarantee you'll make your own day at the same time.

:)

## " True life is lived when tiny changes occur. "
— Leo Tolstoy

JANUARY 8th

# Take the opportunity today to take a step towards one of your lifestyle goals.

You know those lifestyle goals you wrote down on the 1st Jan? Now is the time to start implementing them. If you haven't already done so I suggest you choose one of the goals, then write down the steps you need to take in order to achieve that goal.

Once you have a reasonably concise list, put it in order - what's the first thing you need to do? Then what's the second thing you would need to do etc.

Today is the day to step towards the first one on the list - I've no idea how hard that first step is for you or how easy but do something that moves you along. If it's a tough first step maybe break it down further into another 4 or 5 more steps. Now the first step might be more manageable. Even if you just start making that first step happen today you will have started the ball rolling. And once it's rolling it's easier to build momentum.

Good luck.

> This one was easy for me today as I just needed to write a page of this book - which I have now done! :) (Smug!)

# Take the opportunity to help someone get something they want - Today!

We talk to dozens of people each and every day. Our loved ones, our friends and family, colleagues, acquaintances, shop assistants, fellow dog walkers etc. The list really is quite large even for the most private of us.

Like most of us they will undoubtedly want something, whether it's a new pair of shoes, a new car, new job, relationship, lifestyle etc. the list is as long as there are people you know - believe me!

So, look for an opportunity to help one of the people you talk with today, whether it's face to face, on the phone or via email, and see if you can find a way to help them get what they want. You might find you are the right person in the right place at the right time.

My other half spoke to her friend today and asked if she would like a coffee maker that we hadn't used - she ended up taking a whole bunch of stuff we were trying to get rid of as it turned out she needed them too.
Win - win! :)

# Take the opportunity today to just be still for 5 minutes - Uninterrupted!

This is something most of us don't do at all let alone often enough. If we just spent 5 minutes being still and quiet at least once a day we would find it helps our stress levels which will help our health and well being. It would help us focus on the tasks in hand which will allow us to be more productive - which will relieve stress. It will help us be more creative and in that state of mind we find we can problem solve more readily - and guess what... that will relieve stress.

Try it, and once you get the hang of finding 5 minutes each day, you will start looking for the opportunity to do it 2 times, 3 times or many many times each day.

*"When you improve a little each day, eventually big things occur. When you improve conditioning a little each day, eventually you have a big improvement in conditioning. Not tomorrow, not the next day, but eventually a big gain is made. Don't look for the big, quick improvement. Seek the small improvement one day at a time. That's the only way it happens—and when it happens, it lasts."*

- John Wooden, one of the most successful coaches in the history of college basketball.

## JANUARY 11th

# Take the opportunity today to sing and dance around your kitchen to the bemusement of others!

This will make you feel good for no real reason. I suppose it gets us back in touch with our inner child, remember when you were a kid and you just flitted around making funny noises, pretending you were an aeroplane or a fairy or a superhero. You didn't care who was watching - you were at home!

Find that place again, feel free to express yourself - be a bit barmy. If you can't do it in your own kitchen where can you do it?

Oh, and by the way, if there's nobody else around do it anyway - you'll amuse yourself at least.

*❝ There are times when a man should be content with what he has but never with what he is. ❞*

- William George Jordan

# Take the opportunity today to be kind to a stranger - anonymously.

If you're lucky you'll get to see their reaction. This is a task that when undertaken can really show us that altruism has it's own rewards. You WILL feel good doing something for someone else. The idea of doing it anonymously is to take your ego out of the equation. It's simple to help someone when you get praise for it but more difficult if you will not be recognised for your actions. Maybe you've completed a task at work that someone else took the credit for - smarts a bit doesn't it?

Well in this instance you are consciously making the decision to NOT be recognised for your actions. This way you only have the knowledge yourself that you helped someone. This will give you a bit of a buzz that when repeated over and over will grow. You could become addicted to helping people - wow, wouldn't that be great!

One note: be sure that you're helping and not interfering - it's a fine line sometimes. This one does take a bit of thought and you might not get the opportunity today, but keep it in your mind for the day and I'm sure you'll figure out a way. Putting some money in a charity collector or donating some things to a charity shop are the simplest ways of being kind anonymously that I can think of, but there are as many ways as there are people. Leaving a note on someone's windscreen that their back tyre looks a little flat could be another.

Good luck.

JANUARY 13th

# Take the opportunity today to just say: 'To hell with it!'

Sometimes we're allowed to get a bit frustrated or lose the will to complete something. Sometimes we also worry too much about the consequences, so today see if you can let all that go.

Worrying about that promotion at work? Not today ok.
Housework getting on top of you? Do it tomorrow.
Give yourself a break today from all the hassle in your life and just say: 'To hell with it!'

**" You make progress when you change what you do, not by trying to change who you are. "**

- Ken Christian Ph.D

JANUARY 14th

# Take the opportunity today to start a 'good' habit.

Starting a habit only takes 21 days! That's right, 3 weeks and you are well on your way to creating a good habit in your life whether that's going to the gym every day, eating your 5 a day every day or resisting smoking each and every day.

The next stage is 4 months. If you can push yourself through the first 21 days of creating a habit it exponentially becomes easier and easier each and every day after. When you hit the 16 week mark (4 months) you will have a deeply embedded habit that is harder to stop than it is to continue.

What are you waiting for? Decide today which habit you would like to kick or which you would like to start. Choose one only, in order to give yourself a chance to succeed - you can always choose more habits in the future once you have tasted the success of this first one.

Good luck! :)

---

For quite a few months I have had some issues with my shoulders. I went to the physio and he gave me a set of exercises to do every day. Guess what? I hardly did them at all, maybe once a week. Not surprisingly my shoulder issues persist, so, as of today I started my journey to making those exercises my 'good' habit. I wrote this page and immediately went and did some of them. I wrote a post it note and stuck it on my computer to remind to do them 'every' day.
Woohoo - I'm off and running. :)

---

JANUARY 15th

# Take the opportunity today to call someone you haven't spoken to in a while.

Maybe it's an old friend or acquaintance. Maybe a family member or a previous neighbour. If they spring to mind as you ponder this then take that as a sign that maybe it's a good time to reconnect.

This could also become a healing process if there was a reason for your loss of contact. Be the one that makes the effort to talk again. You might find you missed them more than you realised and vice versa.

I thought about this for a while and struggled to think of someone to call. In the end I went through my mobile contacts list to see if it would nudge me to phone somebody. It did within a few seconds. There was no response. And no response from the second number I called - but hey, third time lucky I got through to a friend of mine. We a had a bit of a catchup then arranged to have supper one evening soon. Result!

## JANUARY 16th
# Take the opportunity today to play.

Maybe you're a playful person all the time, maybe not. Find time to play today in whatever way you can.  And this isn't about playing an instrument. This is about getting back in touch with your inner child and just playing for the fun of it - being silly. Tickle your partner, chase your kids around the house like a monster, be goofy with your friends. Play.

:)

*" The tragedy of life is not that it ends so soon, but that we wait so long to begin it. "*

- W.M. Lewis

JANUARY 17th
# Take the opportunity today to listen to someone.

This is about being there. Not offering advice. Not pointing out someone's mistakes or trying to find a solution for them.

This is simply about listening. We all want to be heard, but how many times do we feel judged or made to feel foolish. We may have been foolish but we don't want our noses rubbed in it, right?

And this is not about pandering to some moaner. We all know them, they're never happy unless they're complaining about something or someone. Avoid those people today and find someone that really needs to be listened to. It may be a work colleague, it may be a friend or family member - it may even be the person on the next table at the coffee shop.

When you listen to someone properly you give them your full attention, you are fully present and it makes them feel valued and important. So turn your mobile off and try and find a time and a place where you won't be disturbed (that's the tricky part!).

When you've fully listened to them you'll appreciate it more when someone really listens to you.

---

I didn't get the chance to do this properly today but I found an opportunity on the 18th when I visited my elderly aunt and uncle in a nursing home. I took the time to sit and listen to them. And, surprisingly they had no interest in telling me about their ailments, they preferred to talk about times they used to go dancing, about other family members and get togethers. I really enjoyed myself and they seemed genuinely pleased to see and talk with me.

JANUARY 18th

# Take the opportunity today to de-clutter ONE room.

I don't have to tell you how good you'll feel once you've done that! De-cluttering once in a while helps us reorganise our minds, our thought patterns and processes. With a clearer mind you'll be more productive in every area of your life.

If one whole room seems a little daunting just do one box - at least it's a start!

Now go get a box!

*" Those who expect moments of change to be comfortable and free of conflict have not learned their history. "*

- Joan Wallach Scott

JANUARY 19th
# Take the opportunity today to do something creative.

If you're a creative kind of person this'll be quite easy. Maybe you'll start a drawing or painting, maybe you'll play something on an instrument, or start knitting a scarf - whatever your particular skill is, put it to task today. Even if you just make a start.

If you find this kind of creativity daunting or intimidating or down right impossible then be creative with your mind. Work out some maths problem, start writing a book, solve a puzzle - be creative about '*how*' you can be creative. Just sitting thinking can be a creative process. All you need to do is give yourself a little bit of time.

## " Crisis is change trying to take place. "

- John Maxwell

> This one is easy for me as I write a page in this book every day - so today my creative thing is writing.

JANUARY 20th

# Take the opportunity today to say something nice about yourself - out loud!

Having a healthy respect for yourself is a prerequisite for being happy, healthy and content. It also gives you the capacity to have respect for other people. When we see faults in ourselves but accept them we are more likely to accept the fault in others.

Saying something nice about yourself '*out loud*' simply reinforces the acceptance. The more senses you can involve in a positive thought the more experiential it will be and the more real it is.

Saying something in your head is one thing, but out loud allows you to audibly 'hear' it *and feel* it (as your mouth moves).

If you want, go write it down too - that way you'll be able to 'see' it. In order to shoehorn taste and smell in there, maybe get a nice cup of coffee, or something good to eat. As you saver the smell and taste, say to yourself: 'This smells and tastes good and I deserve it because...[repeat the nice comment about yourself].

---

I have a couple of daily mantras that I made up about myself, and I try to say these out loud to myself every day. Usually as I get dried after showering or when I'm driving. This is my way of saying something nice about myself out loud. Maybe later on I'll share what they are. Hmm!

JANUARY 21st
# Take the opportunity today to share something.

Could be your time, your dinner, a secret, an intimate moment, your last Rolo - the list is as long as there are thoughts in your head. Have fun with it - do it the whole day if you can. Keep thinking of ways you can share today.

*" To change ones life: start immediately. Do it flamboyantly. No exceptions. "*

- William James

The only sharing opportunity I have had today so far was to share my time and walk my neighbours dog, Grace. My neighbour is poorly at the moment and is under orders to rest (my orders!). So, I had a lot of fun kicking a football around the field whilst Grace chased after it again and again! :)

JANUARY 22nd

# Take the opportunity today to indulge in a lovely memory.

Apart from the fact that this is just a great way to spend 5 minutes of your time this has a secondary purpose. This is a beautiful way to get in touch with gratitude. You can't help feeling grateful whether you're aware of it or not when you remember something that made you feel good. You become grateful for that occurrence as part of the process of enjoying the memory. Think about that as you do this 5 minute exercise. Think about how grateful you are because of that thing that happened.

Enjoy!

Wow! In trying to find one memory I found my mind racing around a whole selection. We met up with a friend of mine from Croatia today which reminded me of a holiday my daughter and I went on some years ago to the island of Rab. I know some people that live there and we saw them while we were there. Even though my daughter was only about 12 at the time she really loved the historical beauty of the place. We swam in the sea and talked in cafe bars over lunch and dinner. It was a lovely week and it reminds how incredibly grateful I am to have her in my life.

JANUARY 23rd

# Take the opportunity today to achieve a small goal.

Depending on who you are this could be anything from resisting a cigarette for the 10th day in a row to flinging yourself out of an aeroplane at 10,000 feet! Me, I'm going to spend a couple of hours with my feet up reading an enjoyable book. I know, that really is a small goal. Having said that, it's something I aim to do quite often and never seem to get around to. Reading seems to be relegated to half hour before bed or maybe twenty minutes at lunchtime in a cafe.

It's a small goal, but it's *my* goal. I hope you find a small goal of your own today that you can achieve.

Good luck.

Well, I managed to achieve my small goal of reading my book for a while. Not for as long as I hoped but longer than I usually manage. So today was a good day. :)

# Take the opportunity today to do something a bit scary!

When we do something scary we step towards our fear, even if it's only a small step, even if it's only a little fear. This is good practise for stepping towards something a lot scarier. This makes it easier to face even bigger fears.

Make a habit of doing something a little bit scary and pretty soon you'll be addressing those fears that have been holding you back from living the life you always dreamed of.

Baby steps lead to toddler steps, which lead to infant steps which lead to hops, skips and jumps - eventually leading to great big enormous leaps.

Take the first step today.

> **66 *Everything you want also wants you. But you have to take action to get it.* 99**
>
> - Jack Canfield

JANUARY 25th
# Take the opportunity today to accept help.

Only when we are able to accept help for ourselves are we truly able to offer help to someone else. It sounds obvious but we can't help someone who doesn't want to be helped. Unless they are ready to *be* helped there's nothing anyone can do. Heighten your awareness to this by accepting help yourself. Practise this and you'll find how and where you are resistant to it, you'll become aware of the signs and possibly the reasons why in some circumstances you don't want help.

I actually missed an opportunity today to accept help. I was collecting some boxes from a supplier and one of the guys there asked if I needed a hand with them, I instinctively said 'No, I'm fine thanks.' Thereby missing the opportunity to help him help me. I did kick myself afterwards. I'll try again tomorrow!

JANUARY 26th

# Take the opportunity today to indulge in an activity that you enjoy.

That's right, treat yourself in whatever way you like. If you want to eat a cake, eat a cake. Maybe you want to go shopping to buy yourself something new. Maybe you want to sit and read a book or enjoy a bottle of wine with a friend. Maybe you want to shoot a couple of games of pool with a friend down the pub or get your nails done.

Whatever you want to do today for YOU - do it.

And enjoy it. You deserve it :)

This was pretty easy for me today, so much so that I indulged in a couple of things that I like. I read for half an hour with a nice cuppa at lunchtime. I had a massage for an hour which was super relaxing and I sat and watched a DVD with a glass of wine in the evening. Lovely!

JANUARY 27th
# Take the opportunity today to do something daring!

Wow, can you do that? Can you be daring? When was the last time you did anything daring? OK, stop worrying, this can be as big or as small as you want it to be. Maybe you'll ask someone on a date - oooh, that's a pretty big one! Or maybe you'll take a 2 hour lunch break. :) You rebel!

Whatever it is, do it today - remember when you get to the end of your life you're more likely to regret the things you DIDN'T do. Make today a day of no regrets.

Ask yourself during today: *'What do I do that's daring?'*

Then ask: *'What could I do that would BE daring?'*

Then do it.

Hey, I'm writing this just to let you know that sometimes when you act daringly it can go completely wrong! But do it anyway! I did something daring that someone found humourous (which is what I intended) but someone else got offended! Ouch! So, I apologised, big deal, felt bad for about an hour - now moving on. Don't let the thought of getting it wrong stop you being daring - make mistakes and apologise to anyone you need to. Onwards and upwards. :)

# Take the opportunity today to make a big decision!

Hmm, are you ready for that? Am I ready for this?

I'm not sure, I spent all day yesterday trying to find something daring to do but nothing came up (although it did a few days later), can I find a big decision that I can make today. Of course it's got to be the right decision. I suppose you and I will *feel* if there's something that needs to be decided. Maybe something has been on your mind for a while - maybe today is the day to grasp the bull by the horns and go for it.

This is a tough one, I realise that as well as you - good luck and wish me luck too.

> **66 Sometimes it's the smallest decisions that can change your life forever. 99**
>
> - Keri Russell

JANUARY 29th

# Take the opportunity today to eat something really GOOD!  :)

That's right - spoil your taste buds today. It could be a healthy meal it could be an indulgent 'not-so-healthy' meal. Just for today treat yourself and eat something you reeeeeaally like. You want choc chip ice-cream? Go eat some. You want lobster thermadore? Go out and get it. You want roast beef and all the trimmings but it's only wednesday? To hell with it, go get a great joint and treat yourself.

All I suggest is that you get the best that you can of what you want. If it's roast beef, try to get ethically sourced, local, organic beef. Lobster or oysters or salmon? Try and get sustainably sourced versions. And if you're on a particular diet at the moment choose the nicest thing that you *can* eat.

Yum yum - enjoy!

## " *I dream therefore, I become.* "

- Cheryl Renne

JANUARY 30th

# Take the opportunity today to look at something natural really close up.

This is a great way to reconnect with nature and reconnect with yourself and all of those around you. When you take the time to really look at something, you notice the little nuances and intricacies that make up the larger whole. When you start doing this with things in nature such as trees or flowers or insects, you will find yourself appreciating it in finer and finer detail. Then you'll find it easier to do with yourself. And when you get used to looking at yourself in minute detail and appreciating every aspect you'll find it easier to do it with everyone and everything around you.

Myself and Em just went to the forest near to where we live. We took our dog Bailey and a friend's dog Grace. In the forest there is a particular tree that, although hollow, is still alive. It must be enormously old as it's easily a five hug tree! (One hug is the distance between your outstretched fingers from one arm to the other.)
I looked at the tree closer and closer, in more and more detail as I drew closer to it. It seems no matter how close you look - something is living, existing, even thriving at that level. There is something ever smaller that is still adding to the whole no matter how closely you peer. I love that!

# Take the opportunity today to review the guides of this month to see which ones you may have missed.

I don't know about you but I find it hard to apply all of the guides on the day. In fact there are some that I've not managed to apply at all yet. So today I'm going to have a look through, make some notes about the ones I haven't done and keep it with me as usual. I'll keep looking at it throughout the day and maybe I'll get the chance to apply at least one of them today.

Tomorrow is a new month so this seems a suitable time to do some catching up.

If by some superhuman effort on your part you have managed to apply every guide so far - give yourself a day off (and a huge pat on the back). Maybe you can review how these guides may have impacted on your life so far? Take a look at the list you made at the beginning and see if you notice any changes. Either way, have a great day!

Something to ponder... did you know that you are not only 1 in 7 billion, but there was in fact only a 1 in 100 million chance of you being You at all? Your father produced approximately that much sperm in order to create you. Only one of those sperm was allowed to win the race to your mother's egg. Think of all the hustle and bustle of that journey. Think of the turning this way and that bumping into countless other sperm. Yet, you managed to reach that destination. All the tiny little changes that sperm made on it's journey enabled it to succeed where 100 million others failed. You already are an incredible success in just being here. See what little changes can do.

FEBRUARY 1st

# Take the opportunity today to ask yourself 'How can I...?'

Bill Harris of Centerpointe fame talks about this in an interview he conducted with Michael Beckwith. The idea is that you consider a block that you have in your life, it might be a career thing, a relationship thing, a money thing. Then you ask yourself: 'How can I find a solution to...?' Your subconscious mind then goes off to find an answer. It actually tries to find the solution for you.

Try it. Start with asking as you fall asleep and see if an answer has come to you in the morning. Keep a notepad and pen by your bed so you can write any ideas or inspirations down immediately.

To learn more about Bill Harris go to: **www.centerpointe.com**

*" It is not the strongest of the species that survive, nor the most intelligent, but the one most responsive to change. "*
　　　　　　　　　　　　　　　　　— Unknown

FEBRUARY 2nd

# Take the opportunity today to be courageous!

This might be in the face of adversity, it might be just being brave about something or it might be something really important like making a difficult decision.

Whether you're nervous about that speaking engagement coming up or whether you need to muster the nerve to ask someone on a date - dig deep and do it. This one courageous moment *could* change your life. Forever!

I know this is one of those difficult challenges I spoke about at the beginning of this book but hopefully you have tried enough of the other challenges to give you some habitual momentum today.

Go for it!

> " *When you blame others, you give up your power to change.* "
>
> - Unknown

FEBRUARY 3rd

# Take the opportunity today to find someone that needs, and will accept, a shoulder rub from you!

Giving a massage is a pure way of giving. It takes quite a bit of energy and work to give a massage - even just a shoulder rub. When you give this to someone wanting nothing in return, when you give this freely you should feel some connection with the recipient. They will feel good, as the touch can be stress relieving, relaxing and loving.

You can save the loving bit for those close to you!  ;)

I managed to find someone who allowed me to give them a shoulder rub. It was my other half so I didn't have to look far. She really appreciated it and that made me feel real good. :)
The thing is I didn't do it today, but got the perfect opportunity after a few days. It was on my mind as I hadn't gone out of my way to make it happen. So if you don't manage to fulfil some of these guides on the actual day, keep them in your mind and hopefully the opportunity will arise at some point.

# Take the opportunity today to read something inspiring.

Most of us have read something that really inspired us. It might have been a novel or self help book, an article or a blog or a news report. When we read these inspiring words we generate thoughts and emotions around them, and in many cases images. This is all powerful stuff because as we go through this process our brain thinks it's actually happening, this is why we can become quite emotional. Our brains don't actually know what's real and what's imaginary. Don't believe me? Give yourself a minute to imagine in vivid detail a ripe juicy lemon. Imagine holding it to your nose and inhaling the citrus smell and feel the dimpled texture of its skin.

Now imagine cutting it in half, holding it up to your mouth and taking a big bite - suck the juice of the lemon into your mouth and swish it around. Hopefully your own mouth is watering right now with the little tingly feeling happening in your jaw.

Reading inspiring words can have a similar affect on how our brains process decisions. You might think certain things are outside of your capabilities - but if you read about someone else with worse circumstances achieving that thing, you are far more likely to rewire your previous thought process.

Read something inspiring every day even if it's just a few sentences and you'll find after a while that you yourself feel more inspired.

I hope you do.

This is my *Be Inspired* blog:

**http://www.conversations-with-blog.blogspot.com**

# Take the opportunity today to look in the mirror and find three things you're happy with.

1. The mirror is clean, 2. the bathroom is airy etc. do not count! :)

I understand this might be difficult for some - I'd even stick my neck out and venture that women will find it harder than men. Try it though and see if you can 'honestly' find three things that you are happy about with your reflection. This could be the start of you appreciating 'you' for who you are. It must start with you, all of your happiness, contentedness, peacefulness etc. comes from loving yourself first.

We've all heard the saying you can't expect someone else to love you if you don't love yourself - so get to it, start today and give everyone else a chance to experience the real you. If you don't know how will anyone else?

FEBRUARY 6th

# Take the opportunity today to recharge the old batteries.

Every now and then we all feel the need to recharge our batteries. The stresses and strains of every day living - especially in the hectic west, can leave us all drained of energy. Just sitting quietly meditating or daydreaming as I like to do, can leave you calm, relaxed and energised. Start with 15 minutes per day if you can. Every other day even. The more you do it the better you'll feel. If you have another method for recharging do that - whatever works for you.

Managed to do this a couple of weeks from now - we spent the weekend doing nothing much. Walked the dogs, read books, watched some TV. We were really lazy and it was great!

FEBRUARY 7th

# Take the opportunity tonight to gaze up at the stars and be awe struck by the sheer size of this universe.

This should be a humbling experience. Whenever I do it, apart from getting a stiff neck, I always feel inspired. Something to do with the magnitude of the universe and the impossibility of understanding how it all got here or even works makes me feel that I don't need all the answers. If my tiny little life is going to mean something I better get on and do something. I realise I must create the opportunities in my life rather than wait around for them to spontaneously appear. This is pretty empowering and I hope you have a similar experience.

Fingers crossed for a clear sky. :)

*66 When you are through changing, you are through. 99*

- Bruce Barton

### FEBRUARY 8th

# Take the opportunity today to find someone who is willing to give you a shoulder rub.

This time you have to actually ask for something for yourself. Yes, you deserve it. If the person you gave a shoulder rub to the other day is not available or able to return the gesture - find someone else. Sometimes you have to ask for what you want and this is an easy one to start with.

> **" If you don't like something, change it. If you can't change it, change your attitude. "**
>
> - Maya Angelou

FEBRUARY 9th

# Take the opportunity today to make someone else laugh.

Bring pleasure to someone's life today by making them laugh - we all know how good it feels and it feels just as good to make some one laugh as it does to laugh yourself. Even better join in and both laugh.

Here's something to get you going:

*"Behind every successful man there is a surprised woman!"*

*"I went to a restaurant the other day that said they served breakfast at any time. So I ordered French toast during the Renaissance!"*

*"My grandfather is hard of hearing. He needs to read lips. I don't mind him reading lips but he uses one of those yellow markers!"*

# Take the opportunity today to say thanks.

This is the simplest thing in the world to do - and sometimes the hardest. We all have occasions where saying thanks to someone really sticks in our side. Sometimes we might even decide not to say it at all. But saying thanks under those conditions can really make a difference, not only to the person you're saying it to, but to *you* too.

When you can say thanks, and mean it sincerely, you are on the path to building a bridge with that person. That relationship could end up growing stronger or at least more bearable.

You can even say thanks to the universe for being just alive!

On the easy side - saying thanks to someone who has just held the door open for you or moved aside to let you through can brighten their day. That thanks will wind its way through the day passing from one person to the next and the next. Be the one that starts that process off and then enjoy the thought of where it might end up. You never know, your easy thanks in the morning could end up being someone else's difficult thanks at the end of the day.

Nice thought huh?

# Take the opportunity today to say YES to something you would normally say no to.

Is this a tricky one? Hmm, not sure. I think some of you might find this difficult depending on what the thing is and how challenging it might be. To others it might be a simple choice of having a cup of coffee after your lunch when you normally don't. Either way, try and say YES - see what happens.

## " *Without change, there would be no butterflies.* "

— Anonymous

FEBRUARY 12th

# Take the opportunity today to spend time with someone that would appreciate it.

We all need some company some times and not just because we're lonely. It may be we need a shoulder to cry on or a sympathetic ear. It may be we could do with a good laugh or a game of chess. Whatever it is, having someone there can make all the difference on occasion. Today - be that someone for someone else.

Today I managed to do this twice! The first time was to spend some quality time with my 21 year old daughter. We went to a book store together then we went and had dinner at a nice restaurant. We chatted and she showed me her latest projects that she's working on at Uni. It was really lovely.
The second opportunity came from sitting with our dog Annie who's just had a leg operation that will see her convalesce in a crate for 6 weeks. She really needed the company - poor thing!

FEBRUARY 13th

# Take the opportunity today to write down a description of your 'perfect' day.

I saw some footage of Frank Kern at an Internet Marketing conference from a couple of years ago, the content is totally relevant to everyone, everywhere. In it he outlines an exercise in which you can find more clarity about your Core (true) self.

The idea is you write down a whole bunch of stuff about your dreams and goals - new house, better job, more money, neat car, perfect partner etc. When you're finished you'll find most of those things reflect the Surface (shell) You. He explains that what we most desire is ongoing 'experience'. Seems obvious, and it is - but sometimes we need to be reminded because we get so wrapped up in our day to day lives that we forget.

Now to get to the Core You go to step 2.

This time, consider your 'Perfect Day'. Imagine it without limitations and without consequences. Write it in as much detail as you possibly can - take some time over it. Start with what would you be thinking about when you wake? What time is it? What's the weather like? What's the view from your bedroom window, who's with you? What do you have for breakfast, and if there's someone with you, what do you talk about over breakfast? Etc. etc. all the way through to your last thought as you lay in the dark about to go to sleep. Imagine you might have to relive this day over and over like Bill Murray in Groundhog day - what would it have to be like for you to be ok with it being like that 'every' day.

When you get to the end of that exercise, read it back, feel like you're actually remembering it from yesterday - how do you feel? Now you should be getting an idea about what the Core You really wants.

(By the way there's a clue about how to identify the Core you - the origin of the word Core means Heart. So look at what your heart is 'feeling' as you imagine your perfect day and it will reflect what you Love.)

To find out more about the brilliant, and [I find] funny, Frank Kern go to: **www.FrankKern.com**.

Beware though, he is a super gifted persuasion expert and he might get you to buy something from him! :)

**" We did not change as we grew older; we just became more clearly ourselves. "** -Lynn Hall

# Take the opportunity today to learn something new about someone close to you.

And before you start thinking about finding their diary I was kind of aiming at finding out experientially or conversationally. Use your imagination. We're rarely closer to someone than when we are in deep intimate conversation with them. Having an honest and open discussion about personal issues deepens understanding and tightens the bonds between us. This should be practiced regularly, maybe you do. If you don't, now's the time to get into the habit. Sometimes these conversations can be a bit uncomfortable but they are always an opportunity to improve your relationships.

What better day to do that than today?

### FEBRUARY 15th
# Take the opportunity today to take 'NO' for an answer.

Sometimes you just have to accept that someone or some situation is not going to go the way you want. Instead of being stubborn and trying to force the issue, try a new approach. Try agreeing to disagree, or try accepting that your way may not be the best way - at least not at the moment. Once you relinquish your desire to control this situation you may find you view it from a different perspective. This may well lead you to view other situations from a different perspective in the future.

Today could be your first day on that journey.

> *" Frustration is NOT created as a result of conditions, certain conditions are created as a RESULT of frustration. "*
>
> -Neale Donald Walsch

FEBRUARY 16th

# Take the opportunity today to stand up and be counted.

You can do this in any number of ways. In stark contrast to yesterday's guide today you may need to stick by your principles/beliefs/ideals etc. You might need to dig your heels in today, stand firm, fight for something you believe in.

Alternatively, you could just defend the integrity of someone else in some way. Maybe somebody needs your support. Maybe your community needs help with local issues. Stick your hand up.

FEBRUARY 17th

# Take the opportunity today to be welcoming.

We all appreciate a warm welcome. We feel valued and loved, pampered and treated. It's just as nice a feeling to be the welcomer, so today go out of your way to be that in whatever capacity you are able. It'll return to you in spades.

*" When we are no longer able to change a situation... We are challenged to change ourselves. "*

- Viktor Frankl

# Take the opportunity today to STOP doing something that doesn't serve you.

So, can you think of anything that you may do from time to time, or maybe even all the time, that you know deep down actually detracts from your own happiness? Dumb question right?

We all have many of these traits, these personality signatures. With some it may be that you eat or drink too much, others may use anger or silence to retain control of situations. Maybe it's even worse - violence, drugs or crime!

With most of us though it manifests in much more subtle ways. You may find you're the type that always wants to be right, you may be shy and steer away from meeting people in case you feel out of your comfort zone, possibly you just have a more negative than positive outlook on life (some call this being 'realistic').

Either way, if you know that behaviour is not serving your best interests, if it's not furthering your growth; spiritually, financially or emotionally, then why not make a concerted effort today to end it. Easier said than done I know - hey I've got my own, but I promise to work on mine if you'll work on yours.

I like to be right all the time - ask anyone that knows me! My stubbornness also holds me back from saying sorry - 'cos that would mean I was wrong! Well, I'm trying to get in to the habit of saying I'm sorry when I've been a bit bull headed or lost my temper with something. I did it this morning with my other half after getting agitated that I was cleaning the house on my day off. My other half correctly pointed out that I was 'choosing' to clean the house. Eventually I apologised for being a grump and the day improved no end. Thanks Em.

FEBRUARY 19th

# Take the opportunity today to get back in touch with your inner child.

There's a difference between acting childlike and being childish. Cast your mind back to a time when you used to play as a child, it could have been with your parents with your friends or just on your own. Remember the sheer joy of playing. They say it's the simple things in life that are most pleasurable and it doesn't get more simple than just playing. When was the last time you wrestled with your partner on the bed? Or had a pillow fight with your kids? Or kicked a ball around with your mates? Or had a water fight with your girlfriends?

If the answer was so long ago you can't quite remember you need to play more. Believe me, these are the things that make life worth living.

FEBRUARY 20th

# Take the opportunity today to do something that makes you feel healthy.

When we do things that make us feel healthy the biproduct is we feel better. Feeling better is a positive thing whenever it happens - obviously, so take every opportunity to feel better. Doing something that makes you feel healthy whether it be going for a jog or a swim, or whether it's eating some good fresh food or taking time to meditate is a habit worth forming. The 'better' feeling we get, can and should become addictive and then you're on a spiral upwards. Start that spiral today.

**" *Change before you have to.* "**

- Jack Welsch

### FEBRUARY 21st
# Take the opportunity today to do something that someone else wants to do.

None of us like to spend time doing things we'd rather not and sometimes it is a waste of your time and energy. Having said that, if it's doing something that someone else is enjoying or maybe even needs to do, then the selfless act of doing it with them can be very fulfilling. Maybe it's as simple as doing something for that person because they *can't* do it.

Anyway, you'll figure out which it is.

> **❝ Nobody can go back and start a new beginning, but anyone can start today and make a new ending. ❞**
>
> -Maria Robinson

# Take the opportunity today to start an affirmation mantra.

This is kind of old school but I think it's well worth doing. I've been doing it for years now and I'm absolutely convinced it has a positive effect on my daily attitude. *"Every day in every way I'm getting better and better."* That's a standard one created by the French psychologist Émile Coué.

At first it might feel a bit silly and a bit contradictory to how you're feeling but stick with it. Do it in the morning and the evening when you are in a favourable physical and mental state. When we tell ourselves we feel a certain way over and over our subconscious begins to accept it as truth. The obvious example is the negative statements some people use; 'I'm so fat.' or 'Nobody cares about me.' or 'I'm stupid.' That's a self fulfilling prophecy right there. As they repeatedly tell themselves those things their subconscious finds reasons to accept it. It recognises the behaviour of people around (which are often negative aswell - misery loves company right!) and reasons; 'Hey, that person agrees with me' or 'That person is horrible to me' etc. thereby making the statements true. Well if it works for negative statements it stands to reason that it'll work for positive ones too. Give your subconscious the idea that you are confident, imaginative, creative, admired, loved etc. and it will find reasons to accept *that*.

You can only give it a go and see for yourself. Try it every day for a month and see if you notice a difference. Farther along I'll give you another technique to use which magnifies the effect, but you need to create the habit first. Start each statement with "I am..." as this puts it in the present tense as if it already *is* that way.

# Take the opportunity today to eat healthily.

This is a no-brainer - when we eat healthily we feel more healthy. We have more vitality, more energy and we generally feel in a better mood which makes us happier. This then makes us better company to be with, more able to be compassionate towards others who might not be feeling as good and thereby improves all of our relationships. You get out what you put in as the old adage goes.

Eat healthily today - then make it a habit.

Being a vegetarian (or pescetarian as I still eat fish from time to time) I do eat pretty healthily anyway. Having said that I managed to cram some more fruit in today as I do neglect that usually. I can't say I feel healthier immediately but I know if I make it a habit I will.

## FEBRUARY 24th
# Take the opportunity today to help a neighbour.

It's a bit of a coincidence that this guide has popped up this morning as I've already had one of my neighbours come around today. She was collecting her spare key as we were looking after her cat and rabbit whilst she was away. In our doorstep conversation she mentioned she didn't get a job she had recently applied for and was now in a quandary as to what direction to next take. I mentioned I had some pertinent information that might help her clear her mind and that I'd send it to her via email.

That's my next task once I have finished writing here.

You might find that the opportunity to help one of your own neighbours needs to be orchestrated somewhat rather than it have fall in your lap. I urge you to consider it, there might be an elderly or injured neighbour that needs some shopping or their grass cut. Someone might need a lift to the doctor's urgently, or even as in my case someone to look after their pet for a couple of days. Extend your hand, put yourself out and help. This is how communities are built and friends made.

Got a warm fuzzy feeling a couple of days after doing this when my neighbour told me how much the email I sent her helped. :)

FEBRUARY 25th

# Take the opportunity today to ask 'why?'

It's only when we ask 'why' that we open ourselves to grow. Whether you receive the answer from someone that knows, whether you just make yourself think about something rather than just accepting it or whether you start a debate about a particular topic, invariably you will learn something.

If we keep learning we keep growing, if we keep growing we keep improving and if we keep improving we stand a better chance of living a more fulfilled and content life.

Oh really? Why?

;)

On the 28th Feb the guide was to revisit any guides I may not have completed at the time. This was one of them. On the 28th I took a phone call from one of Bob Proctor's life coaches and within the hour long conversation I got to ask myself 'why' quite a bit. It ended up being quite revealing. Why do I do certain things the way I do? Why am I not achieving the results I would like in my life. You get the idea. It was a rewarding call and one which I think I will follow up with actually involving myself in the process advised by that life coach. I'll keep you in touch with my progress. :)

# Take the opportunity today to take a step towards a big goal.

We all write these goals down and get enthusiastic about them then sit on them. They stay written down in a notebook or journal or Word Document but more often than not get forgotten about. The busy lives we lead tear us away from those things we really would prefer to be doing.

Trouble is, obviously, without taking any action none of our goals will ever pan out. I suggest, if you haven't already, pick one goal and write down the steps required to fulfil it. Start with the very first thing you'd need to do, then the second and so on. Once you have a pretty comprehensive list go back to the first thing and *do that - today*. If you can get in to the habit of applying the action steps you have outlined you will be reaching your goals before you know it.

Go, go, go...

Of course I could say that just writing this page every day is taking a step towards one of my big goals. But in the spirit of partaking today I have stepped towards a different goal. I am investigating setting up another business - this one will be online. I've been looking at it for a while but today whilst talking about it with my other half I took a step closer to realising what and how I might actually achieve. I've got to tell you I got pretty excited about it! :)

# Take the opportunity today to consider your Triad.

In Tony Robbins' method of Strategic Intervention he talks about the Triad = Physiology + Focus + Language. These three elements are *required* for you to be in ANY state of mind.

*Physiology* describes how you are physically, as in what's your posture, if you're tense ask in which area, the way you are breathing etc. *Focus* examines what you are paying attention to at any moment, what thoughts you're having etc. And *Language* looks at the actual words you use either externally or internally.

So for instance, think for a moment of a time when you were stressed and see if you recognise the following about your possible Triad at that time:

**Physiology**: You were tense in your shoulders and face muscles. Possibly you rubbed your forehead often. Your heart rate went up and you began to breathe more shallowly.

**Focus**: You probably kept thinking of how someone else was going to react to that circumstance. You may have frantically thought of ways to solve that situation so that you didn't seem at fault. You might of even had thoughts that you couldn't do this thing that was causing you stress.

**Language**: You blamed yourself for being stupid or an idiot. You blamed others for causing that situation and that it wasn't your fault? Maybe you questioned why it was happening to you.

Really think back to that occassion, *feel* what it was like - does the above sound familiar?

Well, the same Triad was operating when you had the experience of being on a relaxing holiday. I don't need to give examples of how your Physiology, Focus and Language were different from the stressful experience, but it's pretty obvious they would have been right? (No tension, breathing deeply and slowly, thinking about how this was great to be on holiday away from it all etc.)

So here's where understanding this comes in useful; your mind can only be in <u>one</u> state at a time. Therefore, at any time you find yourself in a negative state of mind be aware of your Physiology, your Focus and your Language. Then, go back to a beautiful experience you had once and relive it with as much feeling as you can. With practice you can change into that more positive state whenever you need to just by remembering your *preferred* state.

Start with altering your posture - this alone will start to take you out of the negative state. When you begin to have doubts about whether you can achieve your goals for instance, imagine your Perfect Day and get back into that state of mind where you understand that *you can achieve everything you want*. Then deliberately change the words you are using to more positive ones. '*I can do this*' or '*I feel calm and in control.*' By changing the three aspects of your Triad you will begin to master your emotions in response to any situation.

Negative emotions are normal but they don't have to be in control. They can't exist without the programmed Triad that established them. Tap into your preffered state today and make a mental note of how your Triad was operating.

To learn more about the incredible Tony Robbins and his distinct style of Life Coaching go to: **www.TonyRobbins.com**

---

FEBRUARY 28th

# Take the opportunity today to review the guides of this month to see which ones you may have missed.

As per the end of January I think this is a good opportunity to step back and take a look at how you got on this month. In case you get the feeling that the guides are running away from you here's your chance to go back and take a look to see which ones jump out at you and shout to be applied.

Take a look at the list you made right at the beginning and see if you notice any changes in your life.

---

Make a note in your journal or diary of any changes you have noticed since you started this book.

---

# My Story

A few years ago I was a disgruntled employee running a print company for someone else. I was on a salary so received no overtime pay. I worked all the hours god sent including 'popping' in most weekends much to my daughter's annoyance, as that was my only time with her. It seemed that there was no way to earn any extra cash as I had no time for another job. Every pay cheque was spent by the time the next one arrived so I had zero savings.

Then I met Mike.

Mike is a hypnotherapist and I met him one saturday afternoon at an open day at a local alternative health centre. I heard him helping a woman who wanted to quit smoking and as I'm interested in all things psychology I thought I'd have a chat with him. Why not - it was free.

We started having a friendly chat and he asked me a question:
*"If you had to think of one thing about yourself you'd like to change what would it be?"*
Well it came out of the blue so I said the first thing that came into my head:
*"I'd like to make better decisions quicker."* I replied.
He then took me through a short question and answer technique ending with putting me in some kind of mind loop - at which time he 'anchored' my request. (A technique to embed that idea in the subconscious)

In total we spoke for about 40 minutes and said our cheerful goodbyes. As I walked down the street however I felt an almost tangible sense of euphoria.

Within 3 months of that experience I had started selling my abstract paintings, something which for 20 years had only been a hobby. I quit my job and started my own business which turned out to be much more lucrative than working for someone - with a lot less hours. Within 18 months I managed to save a hefty sum which I later invested in buying a property to rent out (another business venture). Then I decided to end my 9 years of being alone and set about finding my life partner. Which took another year or so.

One productive period of time! All due to one change. Since then there have been many more changes. I realise now that it's being prepared to make the changes in my life that actually create the difference I'm searching for, so I make changes often. Sometimes small ones, sometimes larger - either way I never know which will have the greatest impact.

So, I get excited by all of them - one at a time. :)


Stu

# Take the opportunity today to forgive someone.

Yeah, I know - that's going to be tough!

Having said that, if you hold any level of resentment or anger or sense of disappointment towards someone for something they may have done, not done, said or not said then consider this today.

I think we all know deep down that forgiving someone (for their trespasses) is the healing thing to do, we know that it will help us in the long run with our own happiness. However, doing it *sincerely* is the hardest thing to do. When we blame someone else for our hurt or the hurt of someone we love, we cling to the idea that we are superior. That in the same situation we would have done it differently. That we wouldn't have been hurtful. That our way of dealing with '*that*' situation would have been better.

Trouble is, even if that's so, even if we would have done things differently, it doesn't make us right and them wrong. They were only doing the best they could from where they were. If that's not acceptable, fine. But if you hold on to that anger or disappointment or resentment you will only damage yourself. It's not good for you - period!

In my experience the way to forgiveness is to first figure out what you gain. What you gain from not forgiving versus what you can gain from forgiving. This is quite confusing to a lot of people as there are so many circumstances in which we can become 'hurt' that it seems crazy to think of ourselves gaining anything from it.

Actually if you look real hard you will always find something is being gained, whether it's the need to feel angry so as to keep guilt or grief at bay, or maybe the deep desire to be 'right' about some occurrence that you can't relinquish your position.

Look and you will find it, sometimes it's buried deep other times it's disguised as something else. But search for the 'gain' and you are sure to find it.

Once identified it becomes so much easier to realise how forgiveness can actually reduce your pain so considerably that it becomes the obvious choice.

Caroline Myss Ph.D author of 'Anatomy of the Spirit' goes in to great detail on this subject - I encourage you to search her out, it'll be worth it.

**If you struggle to forgive ask yourself questions like:**
*'What will I gain for NOT forgiving... [you fill in the blank]?'*
**Then ask:**
*'What will I gain BY forgiving... [you fill in the blank]?'*

# Take the opportunity today to help a charity.

Charities are usually started by well meaning people trying to help some part of our community or wider world. If they're lucky they attract wealthy benefactors but even then they will invariably fall short of funds if they are going to expand their influence.

Fundraising and donating may be the most obvious way and probably the quickest but it's not for everyone. I know a lot of people think that charities waste a lot of money in administration and feel reticent about just giving cash. If this is the case, find one that can prove that the vast majority of funds received are actually spent at the point of need.

Alternatively help the charity in some other capacity such as food drives or clothes drives. Collecting goods that the charity can then either distribute or sell is just as helpful and takes you out of the cash loop. By doing this you also get to experience exactly what you may be achieving in helping.

Giving your time is another great way to help and is restricted only by your imagination. Help in a charity shop one day a week or help by volunteering at a hospice or learning centre or animal sanctuary. Offering your expertise is also a great way to help - if you are good with figures maybe there's a book-keeping role or marketing or procurement or organising events.

There's a multitude of ways to help and all of them will draw you closer to your community, to like minded people and give you a sense of purpose and fulfillment. There's not much in life that competes with the feeling you get from helping others.

# Take the opportunity today to notice something for the first time.

That's an odd one! You might find this one a little bit of a challenge, I mean if you've never noticed something before how do you know *how* to notice it now? Think about it for a moment. Have you ever noticed how you sit when you are using your computer? Have you ever noticed how you greet people that you don't like?

We are surrounded by things and occurrences each and every day that we take for granted. Today, notice at least one of them. It might be something really mundane like how you chop an onion or it might be a little more profound like why you think a certain way about a certain thing.

Oddly, just thinking about *how* you can notice something you've never noticed before will make you notice things all over the place. OK, some of them you may have been aware of but you took no notice of them. That's OK - take notice today.

Notice something today and you'll find yourself doing it all the time. And when you do it all the time there's a chance that you might notice something important that you've been overlooking all these years.

I'm not going to say the word notice anymore - I promise! :)

Remember the old saying: *"Seek and ye shall find."*

MARCH 4th

# Take the opportunity today to help someone feel safe.

Feeling safe is one of main fundamental drives along with food and shelter. So it's not surprising what effect NOT feeling safe has on us. It's not only physical safety we're talking about as in today's sophisticated society insecurity manifests in many ways. Security in our job, security in our relationships, security in our investments.

If you have any influence over someone's sense of security take the time to reassure them today if you're able. It will make a vast difference to their well being.

> " *Security is NOT created as a result of conditions, certain conditions are created as a RESULT of security* "
>
> - Neale Donald Walsch

MARCH 5th

# Take the opportunity today to be BOLD!

There's an old saying that says something like if you want to be lucky in love don't be a wallflower. Meaning: get noticed! (I can say noticed again - it's been a couple of days!) Now I'm not suggesting you change your personality overnight and become super confident and extrovert, I'm just saying be a little bolder than you may usually be. If you are a bit of an extrovert then consider being bold in other ways, maybe find an area of your life that you don't particularly excel at and be bold in that. Maybe you lack confidence in the kitchen - then today say to hell with it I'm going to cook up a feast and *do it*! Maybe you're not great with other people's kids, in which case if not today, then soon - volunteer yourself to play the games they like and really get into it. If they want to go up the park and have piggy-back races grab the biggest one and try and win. It's exhilarating to challenge yourself in those areas you ordinarily feel uncomfortable in - so today, be BOLD!

MARCH 6th

# Take the opportunity today to see the creativity in what you do!

Em and I were talking the other night whilst we walked our dogs about being creative. We debated what it meant to be creative. I was arguing that in order to be truly happy one must be creating. Even the simple single celled organisms live only to re-create. Our deepest desire is to re-create by pro-creating. It's the most natural thing in the system we know as life. Everything that is alive is trying to re-create.

So, maybe if we find ourselves stuck in a job or in a life that isn't in a process of creating we become depressed. After all - this is our purpose. As living entities we are driven to create. Em's point was that simply by tidying her desk she is creating - she's creating a calm space in which to work which might then lead on to more creative thought processes. We debated this point for a while until I conceded that she was right. (It often happens that way!)

So, my point today is we just need to turn our attention to what we are already doing and find the creativity in it. Whether you're an accountant tapping a calculator all day (creating order out of chaos) or if you are a road digger (creating the opportunity for something to be installed or fixed) or a dog walker (creating time to think - for yourself and undoubtedly for the dog owners too), we are all creating in some way, shape or form.

If you feel you are in a bit of a rut at the moment find your creativity - it will reconnect you to your purpose, it may even become your purpose.

Good luck!

MARCH 7th
# Take the opportunity today to write down your career goals!

By writing down our goals we focus on them. When we focus on them we can not only 'feel' if they are actually 'our' goals but also we get to organise them. Organising them gives us the chance to prioritise them and before long you'll be able to realise what the steps are involved in achieving them. Once written, read and ponder them daily. If you just keep them in your mind they don't feel real, they can seem a bit vague at times - you may even forget some of them. Get clear, get focused, get motivated, get a pen!

Now, where's my note pad?

(Once you have written down a list that 'feels' right - extend it. If you haven't already, write down where you want to be in 1 year, 2 years and 5 years. Now get excited about them! If you are doing the 90 Day Program with this book you'll be exploring your goals in depth so use today's guide as a reminder.)

MARCH 8th

# Take the opportunity today to do something for your community.

The selfless act will always make you feel good. Helping an elderly person cross the road, giving directions to someone who is lost or helping a neighbour find their missing cat or dog. All of these will enhance your feeling of worth and value - fundamental aspects of being truly happy. However, helping the community at large rather than just individuals in it can be even more rewarding. Often you don't get the appreciation immediately, sometimes never at all, but internally you will feel the same. Examples of helping the wider community might be volunteering to pick up litter in your local park, helping out at the local youth club, getting involved in the local council or neighbourhood watch. It will take effort on your part but you will undoubtedly make new friends and connections which will enrichen your experience of where you live.

Try it - you'll see. This one thing, if done sincerely, could be the catalyst to change your life in a positive way.

*" A change is as good as a rest "*

- Unknown

MARCH 9th
# Take the opportunity today to write a 'real' letter to someone.

When was the last time you received a letter from someone? I mean a real letter, handwritten, on paper! Think about it. Do you remember? For the purposes of today's guide I suggest you remember a nice letter. Now try and remember how it made you feel to open that envelope and find that letter. It's a great feeling isn't it? In the rush of today's hectic schedules we have resorted mostly to communicating via the internet - Facebook, Twitter, Email etc. and that's fine. It's fun and functional and can be done instantly. But it's not the same as receiving a letter.

Make someone's day tomorrow and write them a letter today. It's a much more robust way of saying I care about you and I'm thinking about you - if for no other reason than it took more time and effort to actually do.

Go get some paper and a pen. You'll enjoy it too and maybe this will become a frequent part of your life. I bet you the person you send a letter to will send a reply the same way - then you'll be the one enjoying opening and reading a letter.

:)

---

I wrote to my grown up daughter, just recounting some old memories of her growing up etc. Two days later she wrote back - I felt great! :)

---

MARCH 10th

# Take the opportunity today to put your foot down if you need to.

A lot of literature in the self-help arena promote being tolerant and understanding, turning the other cheek etc. I'm recommending it right here in this book over and over. But, from time to time, here and there, occasionally - you have to put your foot down about something. You'll know when and what for. Every now and then you really benefit from having something 'your' way. And the people around you will actually benefit from making sure you get your own way now and then. Otherwise you run the risk of being a push over, a doormat, a soft touch. Remember though, this is not about doing it for the sake of it, as I said, you will know when the right occasion presents itself. Just be prepared when it does to calmly stand your ground.

*" One of the most significant findings in psychology in the last twenty years is that individuals can choose the way they think. "*

- Martin Seligman  Ph.D.

MARCH 11th

# Take the opportunity today to forgive yourself of something.

Some of us are holding on to issues that barely bubble below the surface - they're about to burst through at any given moment. The right catalyst is all that's needed - the wrong phrase said at the wrong time by the wrong person can be all it needs to pour out. Usually as anger, often in tears but there are as many ways for it to manifest as there are people on the planet.

Some of these issues are deeper and they vary in intensity but make no mistake, we all have them. Try and identify one of them, start with something pretty small, something that bugs you from time to time but doesn't dog your life on a daily basis. Think about the issue. Remember how old you were at the time it happened, Remember the circumstances that were present. Feel the guilt, then let it go. I know, easier said than done right? Try again, remember as much detail about that issue as you can, feel the guilt that has plagued you since then - then realise that that person isn't you. It 'was' you, but it isn't you anymore. Realise that you have moved on since then, you are different, you wouldn't act that way again, you wouldn't say those things if you were in the same situation now.

We all did stupid, inconsiderate, hurtful things when we were younger, and younger could just mean yesterday, but every day we get the opportunity to change. If you have changed and you can honestly say you would do things differently today then you can forgive your younger self. You might need to go through this process a few times before the guilt goes - or it might disappear immediately. Either way, once you succeed one time, try it again and again with all of your guilty baggage. I promise, you will start to feel a whole lot lighter!

:)

**As before if you struggle to forgive, ask yourself questions like:** *'What will I gain for NOT forgiving myself of...[you fill in the blank]?'*
**Then ask:**
*'What will I gain BY forgiving myself of... [you fill in the blank]?'*

> " **Happiness is NOT created as a result of conditions, certain conditions are created as a RESULT of happiness.** "    - Neale Donald Walsch

MARCH 12th
# Take the opportunity today to accept someone for who they are.

When we accept someone else's failings we make it easier to accept our own. Acceptance is a route towards becoming a happier person as when we accept people we reduce the frustration caused by those traits we disagree with. You'll find that a reduction in your frustration with certain people will actually improve your relationship with them - which then makes it easier to accept them and so on.

*" He who rejects change is the architect of decay. The only human institution which rejects progress is the cemetery. "*

- Harold Wilson.

MARCH 13th

# Take the opportunity today to make a new friend.

Like most people I have a core set of friends. Those that I've known for many years, and some for only a few years. They all have one thing in common. At one point in time I didn't know them!

Obvious I know, but think about it for a moment. If you are invited to a dinner party or other social event or maybe even a work get together and you know that most of the people present will be strangers to you - it puts you off doesn't it? OK, some of you are saying 'No, I love that.' Well this guide today isn't for you, it's for those out there who are happy staying in the comfort and company of familiar friendly faces.

Try to imagine that one of the people you meet today will end up being one of your 'best' friends ever. How great is it to have best friends? It's great, friends that really 'get' who you are and in who's company you can 'be' who you really are. Imagine that one of the people you meet today will be one of those friends and you will have a sense of excitement and anticipation. You won't be able to wait to get out and meet new people.

MARCH 14th

# Take the opportunity today to ask a good question.

Noah St John, author of 'The Secret Code Of Success' encourages us to turn affirmations (positive statements about ourselves) into questions. He calls them *Afformations*.

The idea is that the mind wants to answer questions - it's wired that way. So whilst it's good to say to yourself each and every day:
"I am so happy with my... partner or job or children or level of abundance or whatever." It's actually more powerful an exercise to ask: "Why...am I so happy with my...?" After asking, our mind runs off to go and find relevant information to be able to answer it. It actively searches for evidence of *why* you're so happy with whatever it is.

This is a great exercise and one that I practise as often as possible - one caution though - make sure you keep your questions positive! If you ask: "Why don't I have enough money?" for instance your mind will find the answers and evidence for you. The result might demotivate you instead of inspire you.

To find out more about Noah St. John visit: **www.NoahStJohn.com**

MARCH 15th

# Take the opportunity today to take a step toward one of your career goals.

Hopefully you made a list the other day (7th March) of your career goals. If you didn't get the opportunity then, do it now, today. Make sure you organise it afterwards in to a priority list - it doesn't matter at this time if things will actually pan out exactly as on your list. The important thing is to get the thought process going, the more organised your mind is around the subject the more likely you are to start taking action, and that action will lead to another and another. Be flexible along the way, use your intuition to guide you.

OK, for those of you that have written and organised your list - take the first step to achieving the first one. Whatever it is, do it! As in your other goals, if the first one is actually quite daunting, break it down further in to another 4 or 5 steps. But enable yourself to take a step that will actually start the ball rolling, something that will actually move you 'towards' that goal.

Once you've done it you'll feel fantastic, energised, motivated and inspired. It's worth doing for that feeling alone.

I've had the idea for a while now about having some kind of internet based business. I've dabbled in this and that but nothing ever came of it. To be honest the technology stumps me sometimes and I end up giving up. Today, I realised that I could actually promote this book via the internet once it is finished. So, I started making notes on how other authors in this field are promoting theirs. One small step - but a step.

# Take the opportunity today to help someone else achieve a goal.

Yesterday you took a step towards one of your own goals (hopefully!). Use the strategies that helped you achieve that to help someone else. Obviously they need to be open to being helped - preferably they have actually 'asked' for help. There's usually no point trying to help someone who isn't even in the right mindset to *be* helped.

So, assuming you know someone you can help, suggest they write down their goals and prioritise them - they may say 'Yeah, I know what I want I don't need to write a list', but ask them to do it anyway. Once they pour their goals out onto paper they will have a better idea in which order they want to achieve them (just as you did), then they can put them in order, then they can break the first goal down in to the first steps needed. Before they know it, they'll be on their way to achieving one of their goals and you'll feel great about having helped them.

One piece of advice: don't get attached to the outcome - meaning try not to get frustrated if they don't get on with it straight away, or if they resist the process. We all have our own schedules and timing is 'always' perfect. Just offer your advice then let it go.

# Take the opportunity today to give something away.

How much stuff do we all have?

Answer: A lot!

Take a look around your home - do you see stuff that you don't need or even want. Are there things hidden in draws or cupboards or in the loft that you haven't seen or used in years? Then get rid of them - someone out there can put those things to actual use. They will become valuable again. If you can, give them away rather than trying to sell on, purely because there will be a different feeling attached to the action of giving without receiving anything back.

The best feeling of course is they aren't taking up space in your home anymore.

*" If you don't like something change it; if you can't change it, change the way you think about it. "*

*- Mary Engelbreit*

MARCH 18th

# Take the opportunity today to NOT insist on something.

That's right - let someone have it their way. Even if you know that you are correct it will do you good to just do it their way. Choose wisely, if it's something really important then obviously you need to make a judgement call. When we desist and let someone have it their way we open ourselves to actually seeing it their way rather than arguing against it. If done with authenticity you can't help but try to make it work their way too. You never know, you might end up changing your mind about something.

*" Change is the essence of life. Be willing to surrender what you are for what you could become. "*

-Unknown

# Take the opportunity today to ask for forgiveness for something.

We've all hurt someone in the past. It might have been a loved one, a friend, a colleague or neighbour. It might be the postman or the checkout girl in your local supermarket. It may be small or it may be huge. If you find saying sorry difficult I suggest you start with something small. Once you get into the habit of asking for forgiveness you'll find it easier and easier, then at some point you will find the strength to ask for the big things.

It'll make a difference - to you, AND the person you ask for forgiveness from. Imagine someone that's hurt you in the past approaches you and asks you for forgiveness, they say sorry for the hurt they caused you. They are sincere and they ask you out of the blue so you know they've been thinking about it authentically. What would you do and how would you feel?

If what you imagine is a positive experience consider that you may be the cause of a similar experience if you go and ask forgiveness today. It will make you feel better.


Note: It's possible that the person you ask refuses to forgive you. They may still be hurt. You may have a negative response from them. But let that be OK. The important thing 'for you' is that you've asked. If they're not in the right place yet to forgive you that's down to them. You are only in charge of your own reactions. Remain calm, remain authentic and sincere and you WILL feel better - I promise.

MARCH 20th

# Take the opportunity today to consider Pareto's 80/20 rule in everything you do.

If you're not familiar with this rule it states basically that in any area of your life you get 80% of your results from 20% of your effort. Therefore, if you identify what the effective 20% is, you can do more of that because the other 80% of your effort is a waste of time. Simple but amazingly powerful when you actually apply it.

Start today, apply it in every area and this one thing will make a huge difference in your life.

*66 Change is inevitable - except from a vending machine. 99*

- Robert C. Gallagher

# Take the opportunity today to inspire someone.

I started a blog a while back with the direct purpose of trying to inspire people. I didn't know how I'd do it - I just knew I wanted to. Well it didn't take long for me to start finding things to share that I thought were inspiring; videos, articles, quotes, other blogs - all contributed to my own blog. I found these inspired me to come up with my own posts that hopefully other people found inspiring.

Any time I received a comment either on the blog or via email I felt a rush of enjoyment. When something I said or found and shared inspired someone else I felt great. Helping others is just about the best way to feel good about yourself, so be selfish and help others as much as you can, whenever you can. Inspiring others will be an inspiring endeavour for yourself.

To visit my blog go to:

**www.conversations-with-blog.blogspot.com**

I blogged today about the similarities between bad or unwanted behaviour in dogs and the same in people. I debated that if the unwanted behaviour in dogs was due to some need not being met, could it be the same for people. I hope it inspired some thought for someone.
To read it type this into your browser:
http://bit.ly/ygxaKu

# Take the opportunity today to feel abundant by giving to someone who has less than you.

Neale Donald Walsch said in one of his books that the quickest way to feel a certain way was to enable someone else to feel that way.

So, *you* want to feel more abundant? Your instinct tells you that you need to get more for '*you*', right? Well, that works some of the time for sure, but, if you want to feel it immediately, try the guide. Give a homeless person all the change in your pocket and you'll probably be giving him more than he has already. Your change means a hell of a lot more to him than it does to you. You will feel truly abundant by that person's reaction to your gift. If giving money makes you feel uncomfortable then go buy them a sandwich and a hot drink - the value is the same.

If not a homeless person, then a neighbour or friend or even family member - give them something that they will value and you will feel incredibly wealthy.

Be careful though - this feeling can become addictive! ;)

## MARCH 23rd
# Take the opportunity today to surprise someone.

OK, we're not talking about giving someone a heart attack here! I'm talking surprise them in a nice way - buy them some flowers, take them to dinner, turn up unexpected if you know they'll love to see you, buy them and their other half tickets to the movies - whatever it is, you'll feel great doing it and they will remember you doing it for a long time to come.

There are many ways that you can surprise someone and it doesn't have to include spending any money, let your imagination fly for a while and something will come to mind.

> " If you're in a bad situation, don't worry it'll change. If you're in a good situation, don't worry it'll change. "

> - John A. Simone, Sr.

# Take the opportunity today to identify what really frightens you - then ask why?

On the surface this seems a bit obvious, we're all afraid for our children's safety or walking down a dark alley in a bad neighbourhood and even slasher horror movies.

The fear I'm talking about is more reflective. Are you frightened for your own future, your health, wealth, happiness, job, relationships? Are you afraid of public speaking (who isn't?), or meeting new people. Are you afraid you're not worth it, that you're not capable?

These are deep rooted fears that are very personal, you might not even know you have them, and if you do you may feel afraid or ashamed to share them.

The thing is we all had fears as children, most of which were ungrounded - fear of the dark or the understairs cupboard etc. Once we grew up we were no longer afraid, we knew there was nothing to be afraid of. We became aware.

The same thing will happen now we are adults. Identify your fear, start with a small one. Identify it, see it for what it is, accept it.

This process alone will not magically make the fear disappear but if done repeatedly the fear will grow smaller and smaller, until one day it won't be a fear at all.

A really powerful hypnotherapy technique that helps is to visualise the circumstance that makes you fearful, see it in black & white, then make the image smaller in your mind's eye. Shrink it till it's tiny and far away. You can also use this *disassociation* - by imagining the circumstance as an observer. See yourself in the situation, then allow it to drift into the distance.

It's in the understanding of what's causing our fear where we'll find the awareness to confront it and finally let it go.

This was an interesting exercise for me today. The first thing that came in to my mind was the fear of not being able to do a certain thing. You know the type of thing; I'd like to be in a band but, I don't think I'd ever be able to play good enough. I'd like to start a particular business venture but, I don't think I know enough to do it success-fully etc. etc. Then I asked - why? This was the hard part. After much thought I surmised that it boiled down to security. If I tried one thing, and I put all my energy into it, tried my hardest - and failed! Then what, I would have wasted that time, I'd have to start over on some-thing new - and worry if I'd succeed in that? Probably this is why I have so many projects on the go at any time. It's my way of hedging my bets - if this thing doesn't work out then I've still got these other things on the go. The thing is, when I look back on things I've tried, I've succeeded pretty well. I started my own company which allowed me to earn a lot more than when I worked for someone else. I started selling my paintings and to date have sold a lot, albeit for a fraction of what they're worth. I started buying property and to date now own four. I decided to write this book and so far have writ-ten every day now for nearly three months. So, even though my past successes haven't been of the magnitude of the guru status, I'm no millionaire (yet!), my track record is still one of pretty good success. So what am I afraid of? Wow, and this was only the first thing I thought of. Hmm, I can see this is going to require quite a bit more thought. :)

MARCH 25th

# Take the opportunity today to take a risk.

Get out of your comfort zone - even if it's only slightly. If you're not growing you're shrinking. All things in nature are either growing or dying. When you take a risk you are doing something despite your doubts and reservations. You are facing your fear and doing it anyway. We all live in our relative comfort zones yet we all know that the real sense of 'living' resides in those risk taking endeavours. As time goes by it becomes more and more difficult to take risks because we think we have more to lose. If only we could see that we are 'losing' every day that we don't take the opportunity to grow - and that invariably means taking risk.

I'm not asking you to base jump of your office building or bet your mortgage on the horses. I'm suggesting you identify something you've wanted to do for a while and either do it, or at least investigate doing it. This is a life enhancing activity. When we take calculated risks we feel alive!

After thinking about this for a while and checking back to my reminder a few times - it became apparent what risk I should take today. Why did it take me a few hours to 'see' that something I've been thinking about for many weeks, and that's coming to a head right now and contains risk, wouldn't spring to my mind immediately? Just shows the power of having a guide written down. The power of reading it and considering it over and over. Sometimes the answer is right in front of us. Well, after some further thought this morning I am going to take this risk - if it works it will be another step in the right direction for me and I'll probably repeat it in the future. If not - I will at least have learned something. :)

MARCH 26th

# Take the opportunity today to do something completely selfless.

Allow your altruistic self to be active today. Try and think of the best for others the whole day. Do what they want to do. Enable them to get what they want. Go out of your way to help. The reward will be apparent.

> **" There is a certain relief in change, even though it be from bad to worse! As I have often found in travelling in a stagecoach, that it is often a comfort to shift one's position, and be bruised in a new place. "**
>
> - Washington Irving

MARCH 27th

# Take the opportunity today to go for a walk in nature.

Reconnect today with the natural world. I don't know anybody that doesn't enjoy walking in the woods, or strolling in the park, or hiking across the countryside from time to time. It's when we immerse ourselves in nature we feel 'natural'. It's in this realisation that we are not part of some concrete mega life but actually an inter-connected organism just like any other on this planet that we get a taste of our true selves.

Trust it, enjoy it, embrace it - then you'll ask why you don't do it more often.

## " *Growth is the only evidence of life.* "

\- John Henry Newman

# Take the opportunity today to give yourself permission for something. You know what it is.

We've all got things lurking in the back of our mind that we'd like to do but feel we shouldn't or couldn't. These feelings are usually manifestations of guilt or inferiority. The list of what these things could be is infinite but here are a few examples:

A. You want a promotion at work, but it would mean being the boss of some of your colleagues and you're worried they will behave differently towards you; or,

B. You'd love to play in a band but learning an instrument at your age would be embarrassing and really difficult; or,

C. You'd feel great driving a flash sports car for a while but you think it's egotistical; or,

D. You want to stop doing something you feel you are made to do but you think people will regard you as selfish;

etc. etc.

Figured out what it is for you yet? Give it some thought - then give yourself permission. You will feel invigorated and empowered. Remember though, other people's reactions just need to be accepted, use your intuition to decide whether they have any merit.

MARCH 29th

# Take the opportunity today to find a compromise.

Finding a compromise means seeing the other person's view. It doesn't mean agreeing with it, it just means acknowledging it. This shows you have respect for that point of view and therefore respect for that other person. We all want to be respected, it means we're valuable and valued. You want to feel that way - so allow someone else to feel that way too.

You never know, you may actually end up changing your mind about something. :)

*66 When you are through changing, you are through. 99*

- Bruce Barton

MARCH 30th

# Take the opportunity today to let someone else have it their way.

This sounds a bit like yesterday's guide - but it isn't! Yesterday hopefully, we compromised, we found a middle ground. Today let's just let it go. Whatever it is you're able to let go but seem to be hanging on to. Let it go. Let someone else win. Believe me, this thing is a burden to you. Let it go and you will actually feel relieved.

*" If you don't like something change it; if you can't change it, change the way you think about it. "*

\- Mary Engelbreit

MARCH 31st

# Take the opportunity today to review the guides of this month to see which ones you may have missed.

As usual on the last day of the month let's take the time to go back and see if there are any guides that have been missed, forgotten or just haven't happened. I certainly don't manage to do every guide on the day. Tomorrow is a new month so this seems a suitable time to do some catching up.

Review how these guides may have impacted on your life so far? Take another look at the list you made at the beginning and see if you notice any changes. Either way, have a great day!

---

Make a note in your journal or diary of any changes you have noticed since you started this book.

---

As if it needs emphasising I wanted to share an idea with you. I was watching a program on the BBC recently called 'Everything and Nothing' by Jim Al-Khalili. It explains our most up to date theories on what 'Everything' is and also what 'Nothing' is. The relevant part was the notion that at the beginning of the universe there were tiny fluctuations in the vacuum of space. We're talking billionths of a second after the big bang and fluctuations trillionths of the size of an atom here! Apparently it was these tiny minuscule fluctuations that went on to cause the formation of galaxies. Something that incredibly tiny caused something that incredibly big. See what small changes can do.

APRIL 1st

# Take the opportunity today to not take yourself so seriously.

Here in the UK April 1st is 'April Fool's Day'. It's a morning of practical jokes and pranks that we do on each other - just for fun. Even the BBC joins in - one year they had a report about how to harvest spaghetti from a pasta tree!

Whilst some people can perform a joke that is cruel or spiteful (which is not in the spirit of the day) most are just good fun. The point is to laugh at yourself. Allow yourself to be caught out. Be the object of humour. Then pass it on :)

(Make sure it's before midday though otherwise the joke's on you!)

APRIL 2nd

# Take the opportunity today to get rid of something that isn't either functional, beautiful or personal.

In the same vain as decluttering find just one thing today that you don't need or want. We all have them. In fact we all have many of them. My other half yesterday sorted through our kitchen pots and pans and utensils and found a whole load of things we have two or more of. She has taken them to her young cousin who is starting Uni soon. They're going to a good and appreciative home where they'll be used and not left in the back of the drawer or cupboard for years. Your own items could come from your kitchen or your wardrobe or your garage or your attic or... you get the idea.

Once you have managed it with one item there'll be no stopping you. Careful though - apply the three guides in the title above before getting rid of anything. At the end of today you WILL feel lighter - even if you're exhausted.

# Take the opportunity today to look through some of your old photos.

Since photography was invented the miracle of capturing a moment in time touched people deep inside. The possibility of being visually taken back to a memory became priceless. Soldiers went to battle with a picture of their loved ones - the most valuable item they owned at that moment. Those photos defined them. The fallen enemy soldiers wallets would contain the same cherished images.

We all love the photos we own even though we're in the film age, even though it's so easy to look back at videos - photos retain their intrinsic value. Once you have a photo you don't need any device to play them on. You just need eyes to see.

Replay some of those old memories, beautiful heartfelt moments, funny laugh out loud moments, deep and meaningful moments. Reconnect with who you are and what has shaped you through the miracle of your old photos.

OK, that was nice. The funniest thing is looking at the hairstyles - oh dear! It has made me want to get in contact with some old friends in the photos that I haven't seen for a long while.

APRIL 4th

# Take the opportunity today to admit something about yourself to yourself.

Hmm, this will be interesting. This is going to take a little bit of self analysis for most of us. Maybe you are very aware of some things about yourself already, in which case I challenge you to look a little deeper and figure out why you're like that. For the rest of us, ponder it during the day. Maybe you'll admit that you're angry about something. Maybe you'll admit you're disappointed about something or lazy. There really are an infinite amount of things that we could admit to ourselves about who and what we are.

However, remember these things can be positive aswell as negative. We all find it easy to be self critical, which is our way of recognising our shortcomings so we can deal with them - hopefully. Some of you are in this state far too often on the other hand and could well do with admitting something very positive about yourself. Maybe you can admit that you are very generous. Maybe you are incredibly loyal and honest and trustworthy. If this is you, remind yourself today.

Either way this is a cathartic process to go through but it will take some thought and some effort.

---

Amongst the many things good and bad I noticed one in particular - I don't practice what I preach often enough. I will make a concerted effort to do so more from now on.

---

APRIL 5th

# Take the opportunity today to listen without judging.

If you think about this for a moment you'll probably realise that a lot of the time you're listening to someone else you're not actually listening. Hearing someone and listening to someone are completely different. Usually this is happening when you are having a disagreement or argument. You are so focused on getting your point across (listened to) that you don't seriously consider what the other person is saying. I can remember many, many times in this situation where I was just waiting for the chance to say what I wanted to say that I didn't even care what the other person's point was.

If this sounds familiar to you - and I'm sure it does, then consider 'listening' today. Understand what the other person's point or frustration is. Really see it from their shoes, then see how that makes you feel and think. Your response will be more authentic, understanding, compassionate and meaningful.

This doesn't however mean you have to agree with the other person. At the end of the discussion you can calmly acknowledge their standpoint and agree to disagree.

---

I found myself in conversation with a friend this evening. He was saying that he truly believed in fate and that our lives were all mapped out. I immediately defaulted to judging this comment and debated about the science of that theory. After a while I remembered to listen without judging. The conversation changed. We investigated what mechanisms might be in place to actually allow that possibility. Although it's still not my belief I found that opening to at least the possibility allowed my mind to be more creative than combative. It was a more enjoyable conversation because of that. :)

---

APRIL 6th

# Take the opportunity today to cook your favourite dinner.

I don't know about you but I find cooking therapeutic. It's like meditation, especially if it's something I've cooked many times before because then I'm on autopilot and my mind just drifts off. (Helps to have a good glass of Rioja on the go too!) Whether you enjoy cooking or not, most of us can cook at least one meal that we really enjoy.

Cook that one tonight, allow it to absorb you. Fully immerse yourself in the process. Then see where your mind goes.

Enjoy your evening. Yum Yum! :)

**❝ It is not necessary to change. Survival is not mandatory. ❞**

- W. Edwards Deming

APRIL 7th
# Take the opportunity today
# to invite someone to dinner.

When I was younger I used to love going out socialising, down the pub mostly. The drink would flow and we had a lot of fun. Nowadays, I'm a bit more mature (some would argue with that statement!) and as much as I still enjoy an evening down the pub or at a nice restaurant, albeit a much quieter event - I really enjoy socialising at home. There's more of an informal atmosphere, you don't have to worry if you're being too loud and you don't have to worry about getting a cab back.

Inviting people to dinner is also a very primeval thing to do I think. One of our greatest survival drivers is to find food. I'm sure at an early stage in civilisation providing food for other members of our tribe was an incredibly bonding experience. That same bonding experience is still there in our psyche, we might not be so aware of it, but it is. At the very core of it you are saying 'share in all we have' to your friends and family. It's an amazingly generous gesture.

APRIL 8th

# Take the opportunity to kick a habit, starting today!

Every journey they say, starts with a single step. Take that first step today to kicking a habit you don't like or you realise doesn't help you. Psychological studies have shown that unless you continue along a course of action for four months you won't embed that action as a habit. The hardest part of that process is the first 21 days. What I have found also is that unless you substitute a bad habit with a good one, you will actually start a new bad one.

So, if you want to kick smoking for instance, and say you smoke 20 per day, rather than stopping today and saying 'that's it no more cigarettes ever', change the habit to smoking one less cigarette per day. By the time you get to 21 days you will have actually got down to zero cigarettes - this is now your habit. Now do that for four months.

What also might help, is every time you fancy a smoke use the time to walk somewhere (without your cigarettes). Five minutes walking every time you want to smoke will actually become your good habit.

# Take the opportunity today to read a good book!

All you book readers out there will thinking "Mmmmm" - oh yeah, sit in a nice comfy place, maybe a hot cup of something or maybe a glass of wine, and lose yourself in something entertaining, intriguing, fascinating, enthralling or all of them put together.

Non-book readers out there will probably be thinking they'd rather be fiddling with some gadget, or maybe doing some kind of craft work. Well if that's what takes your mind away do that. It's about getting away from the hustle and bustle of your everyday mind. So, whatever you do for that - do it.

I'm going to guess that most of you like reading - as you're reading this!  :)

> **" All changes, even the most longed for, have their melancholy; for what we leave behind us is a part of ourselves; we must die to one life before we can enter another. "**

— Anatole France

APRIL 10th

# Take the opportunity today to randomly choose a recipe from one of your least used cook books and prepare That for dinner.

We've all got them haven't we? Cook books gathering dust. Cook books that you can't remember the last time you even looked inside. We are creatures of habit every one of us. Today's guide is aimed at just getting you to dip a toe outside your habit zone. Ignore the 10 - 20 things you normally cook and do something different. Let some new flavour in to your life. Look at the shelves in the shop a little differently. Ponder the vast array of choices we are lucky to have.

Remember though, this is not about buying expensive, exotic fare, although if that's what takes your fancy then go for it. A simple inexpensive leek and Tarragon rissotto could be a taste sensation you will wish you had tried years ago. Changing our daily routine in as simple a way as what we have for dinner can sometimes be a catalyst for other changes. Give it a try and I hope you enjoy dinner tonight!

I looked through a Spanish cook book that I have and found a dish called Sofregit (it means to fry lightly), and although all the recipes were for chicken or pork or fish, I adapted it to make a vegetarian version. Yum!
I think it will now become one of our feature meals.
Having said that I enjoyed the process so much that I'm going to make a habit of searching my cookbooks for new recipes.

APRIL 11th

# Take the opportunity today to celebrate something - anything!

We celebrate birthdays and religious holidays and anniversaries and special days throughout the year, but then slip back in to our everyday lives 99% of the time. When I was a kid I used to think it would be great to have Christmas every day - why not? It was fun and everybody was in a good mood. Obviously, I didn't realise that what makes Christmas 'special' is that it only happens once a year. However, there's nothing to stop us celebrating something else on the other days. How about - it's just great to be alive!

I'm not saying celebrate something every day (unless you want to), I'm saying celebrate 'any' day. Just choose something to celebrate because it'll lift your mood, or reconnect you with friends, or cheer someone else up. Here's a few examples:

Happy Graduation Anniversary

Share A Cuppa Day

Cakes Have No Calories Day

I've Completed That Task I've Been Doing For Ages Day

A Hot Guy/Girl Smiled At Me Day

It's Only Two Weeks To My Holiday Day

You get the idea. Have fun with it, then anytime you feel like you need a special day just create one. :)

I put this page on my blog at the time and was amazed at how the idea of 'Cakes Have No Calories Day' was so universally enjoyed! :)
Here's a reminder of my blog:
**www.conversations-with-blog.blogspot.com**

# Take the opportunity today to explain all the events that happen to you, to your favour.

It's widely considered that our subconscious minds can't actually discern what's real and what isn't. This is how hypnosis works. You put a suggestion in and it's accepted as true. So, today, whatever happens to you or around you take a moment to make up a reason why that thing is good for you. If you trip on the pavement and spill your cappuccino, say, that was lucky - I didn't really want that coffee anyway as I'm trying to relax and that would have fired me up. Or, if the train home is delayed, say, excellent I get a bit longer to unwind from work before I get home and I can read a bit more of my magazine.

Get the idea? Remember to try and 'feel' that your explanation is true in order to give your subconscious the reason to believe it.

Try it. It's fun and you'll be in a better mood about all of those things that ordinarily might annoy you.

APRIL 13th
# Take the opportunity today to be spontaneous.

For the most part most of us plan plan plan. We get up, have breakfast, get ready for work, leave in time to get the train. Work a full day, leave around the same time, maybe go to the shop to get dinner supplies. Go home, cook, eat - maybe even plan to meet up with friends. That's good for most of the time. Planning makes us more efficient, without it society would collapse.

But, sometimes we all need to get off the treadmill. Close the diary, stop checking our watches and clocks, and change direction. Even if it's only for a couple of hours. When we do this we feel that we are in control. We feel that we are guiding our own life. We feel like we are 'living'.

It's a great feeling - so treat yourself. Be spontaneous more often, starting with today.

When I feel the need to be spontaneous I usually jump in my car and go explore somewhere I don't know. I usually find pubs or churches or restaurants or parks or woods that I never knew existed. I found my previous home by doing exactly that - it was in a village miles from where I lived at that time and I fell in love with it.
When you're spontaneous you never know what's going to happen - I love that!

APRIL 14th

# Take the opportunity today to see it from their shoes.

More often than not we find ourselves (I certainly do anyway) defending our point of view in a discussion. It's one of my many personality flaws - I like to think I'm always right! But if we can stop just for a moment and really put ourselves in the other person's shoes we can get a look at the bigger picture from a different angle. It's through practising this exercise that we can empathise more, understand more fully and appreciate the other. Try it and I think you'll find you're relationships become stronger and more respectful.

I know because I'm always right!  ;)

> *66 Without accepting the fact that everything changes, we cannot find perfect composure. But unfortunately, although it is true, it is difficult for us to accept it. Because we cannot accept the truth of transience, we suffer. 99*

- Shunryu Suzuki

126

# Take the opportunity today to try and understand something that upsets you.

*'You're never upset for the reason you think.'* That's the title of Paul and Layne Cutright's #1 Amazon Bestselling book. It explores the root causes of why we are upset, presupposing that what we think we're upset over is in actual fact a guise for something else completely.

If you find yourself getting upset over all sorts of things it's possible they *all* have the same root cause. Once you identify that, you are well on your way to alleviating some, if not all, of the feelings associated with it including: anger, hurt, defensiveness, blame, guilt, shame, confusion etc.

If you do suffer from constant upset this exercise could seriously improve your life. Start by asking yourself: 'What else could I really be getting upset about here?' Just explore the possibility. It takes being brutally honest with yourself, are you ready for that?

APRIL 16th
# Take the opportunity today to use the rubber band method.

Huh? What's that? - I hear you ask.

Go get a rubber band, one that will comfortably fit around your wrist (make sure you can wear it all day without restricting your blood supply!). Done that? I'm going to presume you have.

Now, as you go through the day and you find yourself having a negative thought - it could be about how many phone calls or emails you are getting, or about how the paperboy has torn your paper putting it through your letterbox, or maybe frustration at the train being late, or having a negative thought towards a coworker. Whatever the reason, it's not important, if you notice the negative thought - snap the rubber band against your wrist.

What's happening is similar to the Pavlov's Dog experiment. Pavlov managed to get a dog to salivate at the sound of a bell by first feeding the dog at the sound of that bell over and over. So, the snapping of the band is there to give you an uncomfortable experience which you will associate with the negative thoughts. After a while the first moment of a negative thought will make you want to change your thought to something more positive. When you notice that happening you can dispense with the rubber band.

Happy snapping!

APRIL 17th

# Take the opportunity today to try and understand something that confuses you.

I'm confused by a lot of things. Women mainly! ;)

Seriously though, I'm not really talking here about getting to grips with Pythagoras or the stock market or how building roads reduces inflation. I'm talking about things like why do you choose the partners you do, or why don't you get the promotion you deserve, or why do you never get time to do the things you want?

When you look at those things you'll probably find yourself going around in circles for a while - I don't get promoted because my boss doesn't like me, for example. When that happens interject the word *why*. So, my boss doesn't like me - *why*? It's because he knows I can do the job better than him - *why*? Because I've been doing this for 10 years and know it inside out - *why*? (wouldn't your boss find that valuable)....Er, hmm. He would wouldn't he? Now you start getting somewhere. Now start asking why, in a more discerning way - if my boss would find that valuable why won't he promote me? Now you can get deep and you'll probably uncover some little doubt in your own mind. Some little fear of change that stops you behaving in a way that would convince your boss to promote you.

This is a tricky one I know, it's going to take you some time with a bit of peace and quiet. But you'll find it useful if you're prepared to look inward for the answers rather than outward for the excuses.

APRIL 18th

# Take the opportunity today to be aware if you're tense.

Most of us will become tense throughout the day under certain circumstances. Whether we're sitting for too long at the computer or stuck in traffic or trying to concentrate on a task. At these times muscular tension can manifest. If it continues for too long we can suffer from headaches, back aches, muscular pain, neck pain to name just a few. I'm sure we're all familiar with those!

Taking a moment to be aware of your body throughout the day gives you a chance to relax those tense areas. The more you practise taking a moment to ask yourself if you are tense the more rapidly you will begin to notice it *as it happens*. Before long you will be able to do this subconsciously and you'll have a lot less aches and pains.

That's got to be a worthwhile life change.

APRIL 19th
# Take the opportunity today
# to stretch.

How often do you stretch? If you're like me - not very often. I train once a week and that's when I do my stretching. I feel good afterwards. I feel looser, more supple, more energetic and more alive. So, why don't I do it every day? I use the same old excuse of 'I don't have time.' Well that's plain dumb! I'm going to make time. 15 minutes per day is plenty, if I can't find 15 minutes per day then I might as well order a zimmer frame right now!

So I encourage you to do the same starting today - it'll make you feel so much better and the process itself releases endorphins which make you feel happy too.

Start streeeeeeeetching today!

---

So, you remember a few days ago I said I don't practice what I preach - well I came back to this page at the end of the month when I reviewed those guides which I might not have completed and guess what? Yep, I hadn't stretched apart from my usual Tuesday training stretch. So I just did 15 minutes stretching. I stopped what I was doing and stretched. Surprise surprise, the world hasn't stopped. There have been no disasters. It seems that taking 15 minutes out of my day is actually pretty easy. Now to make it a habit.

APRIL 20th

# Take the opportunity today to understand something that makes you angry.

Where do I start I hear you say. Well you know what, that means this should be easy. If there are so many, just pick one randomly. Maybe the dustbin men make too much noise too early in the morning. Maybe your neighbour doesn't pick up after his dog fouls the pavement. Maybe your boss treats you like a servant.
Whatever it is just pick one. Got one? You want that one? OK!

Now, apparently anything that makes us angry is based in fear. I know, I know, you're not afraid of the bin men. It's not that kind of fear. Let me add this, apparently any criticism of another is really a criticism of ourselves. So, you might be angry at those bin men for being inconsiderate in making so much noise so early - ask yourself what you think you might be inconsiderate about. Now ask yourself if you might be afraid to be thought of as inconsiderate - we're not talking shaking in our boots here, we're talking concerned, worried or anxious. (All of which are levels of fear.)

Ponder these ideas today and you might get to the bottom of why something makes you angry. Once you understand it you generally find the anger is diluted, if not removed all together.

---

I really get angry if I'm clumsy. It doesn't bother me so much if other people are clumsy. So why do I get angry if I'm clumsy? After a little ponder I came to the conclusion that being clumsy was a result of rushing or not taking enough care or not concentrating. These are traits that I don't like as they seem ignorant, out of control or plain lazy. And when I display clumsiness I brand myself with those traits. From now on I'll try to take more care etc. and hopefully be less clumsy.

# Take the opportunity today to understand something that fills you with joy!

Do you know what fills you with joy?

It could be holding your loved one close. It could be holding one of your children in your arms or watching them enjoy themselves. It could be driving down a country lane with the roof down and the wind in your hair on a summer's day.

Whatever it might be, consider it for a moment. I mean really think about it right now. Imagine it. See it happening right now. That feels good doesn't it? Now try to understand why. It might seem obvious at first but give it some thought and ask yourself: 'Why does this fill me with joy?" The answer might be revealing. Even if it's not it'll make you feel good just to think about it.

:)

> **" At any moment, the decision you make can change the course of your life forever. "**
>
> - Anthony Robbins

APRIL 22nd
# Take the opportunity today to write a letter from the 110 year old you to the you of now.

This guide is thanks to Brian Johnson author of 'A Philosopher's Notes' - the idea is that the old you only has 60 seconds to give you some advice about life. Based on Tal Ben-Shahar's psychological exercise which helps us understand that we already have all the wisdom we need. Tal Ben-Shahar used evidence of near death individuals that used their experience to go on and live very different lives.

What pearls of wisdom could the 110 year old you impart? What do you think You from the far future would tell You of now if you had just one minute?

I think this is what my 110 year old self would say:
'You know what Stu, you only get one time around. Get on with whatever it is you want to do. Be who you want to be. Be cautious not fearful. Be bold not reserved. Go for it because you can't fail. You can only experience and learn. As long as you get back up after a fall and try again. But most of all LIVE! Smell the roses, sip the wine, enjoy your friends and family as often as you can and be brave.'
Easier said than done? Of course. If it wasn't everyone would be doing it. Starting today I aim to be one of the ones that LIVED. What about you?

APRIL 23rd

# Take the opportunity today to party.

We all need to let our hair down - do that today.
And if you can't do it today, at least plan it today. :)

*" Your time is limited, so don't waste it living someone else's life. Don't be trapped by dogma, which is living with the results of other people's thinking. Don't let the noise of others' opinions drown out your own inner voice. And most important, have the courage to follow your heart and intuition. They somehow already know what you truly want to become. Everything else is secondary. "*

- Steve Jobs

APRIL 24th

# Take the opportunity today to slay one of your Dragons.

Our wardrobes are full of monsters from our childhood which manifest themselves as Dragons in our waking hours. It might be the Dragon boss who moans if you're one minute late. Or it might be your Dragon neighbour that constantly creates tension over the back fence. Or maybe it's your fear Dragon that jumps out on you when you're about to do something challenging.

To slay your Dragon you need only to confront it - not with a lance like St. George! Rather, with an assertive mind or a well chosen word. Apologise to the boss for being late rather than offering an excuse - offer to stay five minutes on for every minute you were late. Ask your neighbour around for coffee, ask them what you might be able to compromise on so that you can get on better. Most importantly, feel your fears and do it anyway as Susan Jeffers says in her book of the same name. It'll make you stronger.

*" The only thing to fear is fear itself. "*

- Franklin D. Roosevelt

# Take the opportunity today to write out your health goals.

I know I've got plenty of these and I'm guessing you have a few too. Just like setting any other goal, writing them down, then putting them in priority order is actually a large step towards achieving them. In the process of writing them you will probably come up with ideas of how you can implement changes that will help you towards them. At that point you have the ball well and truly rolling.

Do it now - do it today because you ain't got nothin' if you aint got your health.

*" Any change, even a change for the better, is always accompanied by drawbacks and discomforts. "* - Arnold Bennett

# Take the opportunity today to bite your tongue.

Can you remember a time when you said something then wished you hadn't? I know I can. I'm quite a challenging person at the best of times. I hope that for the most part that it's well intentioned. However, sometimes it's not well received. Sometimes the person being challenged doesn't want to go through the process.

Sometimes they just want some sympathy and understanding. I've hurt people's feelings in the past by being more interested in my point of view than their feelings. Once hurt it's hard to retract what you've said. It will stay with that person long after you've apologised.

So, today, if you get the opportunity to challenge someone - STOP! Take a moment to consider the situation. If you feel that the other person is just about ready to explode or burst into tears or storm out of the room - bite your tongue. Swallow those words you were going to utter and regurgitate some softer ones.

# Take the opportunity today to take a step towards one of your health goals.

If you got around to writing down your health goals the other day take the time to do something about it now. If you were going to join a gym but haven't done it yet - go get the Yellow Pages. If you were going to improve your diet start today to ditch the junk.

Pick a goal and figure out what the very first thing you need to do to step towards it is - then do it! If you haven't written your goals yet, do it asap. In the meantime think of one thing you could do right now to improve your health. Thought of it?

Good! Now what's the first step towards that?

Great - now do it!

If not now then when?

# Take the opportunity today to write out a list of your hobbies.

It's good to remember what you enjoy doing. Once you start writing them down you'll be surprised at how many hobbies you have. Then you'll start to realise that you hardly spend any time indulging in those hobbies. Remember those are the things you like to do in your spare time. If you won the lottery tomorrow you could spend all day doing them. Well why wait until you have more time? Stop doing some of the dull boring things that take up your spare time at the moment and start indulging more of that time doing the things on that list.

Life's too short to waste it doing stuff we get no joy from.

APRIL 29th

# Take the opportunity today to indulge in one of your hobbies.

If you took the time to write a list of your hobbies yesterday - indulge in one today. If you don't have much time today choose one that won't take long. When we were children we had all the time in the world. Most of our spare time would be spent partaking of our hobbies. Then we grew up and got busy. Make time to enjoy those things that interest you, imagine reaching old age and realising lots of the things you used to like to do were no longer available to you. If you like playing squash you're going to find that difficult if you wait until you're 65 years old!

I didn't have much time myself today so I just played a game of chess against my computer. I lost! Then again, I always lose against my computer - I seem to have it set on invincible! Nevermind, I enjoyed playing.

APRIL 30th

# Take the opportunity today to review the guides of this month to see which ones you may have missed.

As usual on the last day of the month let's take the time to go back and see if there are any guides that have been missed, forgotten or just haven't happened. I certainly don't manage to do every guide on the day.

I usually leave the reviewing until the weekend unless I get some time during a weekday evening. It takes a bit of peace and quiet if you're going to try and do as many guides as possible. Try though, I guarantee it'll be worth it.

---

Make a note in your journal or diary of any changes you have noticed since you started this book.

---

# Claire's Story

Sometime's it feels like you have to make Herculean efforts to change your life when you're not happy with it, especially if you are having a tough time or if you feel life has given you a raw deal. After a terrible year where I felt stuck in a rut at work, when the bank put up our mortgage when everyone else's was coming down and when both of our cars blew up and we couldn't afford to replace them, I didn't feel like I had the inclination or energy to 'look on the bright side'. The most I could manage was a cup of tea and a whinge with friends. It was when I was sat down with Stuart and his partner Emma, something clicked when they gently asked me 'why do you like being unhappy?'. I was a little taken aback at first and then realised (to my horror) they were right – I was solely focused on the negatives. It was easier to be a bystander in my own life and accept the raw deal, than it was to do something to change it for the better. By only looking at what had gone wrong and taking a 'woe-is-me' attitude, I was handing off my own future and letting others control it.

My friends' kindness and frank and honest comment challenged me and made me realise that although bad things happen at times, it's not something I was prepared to let define me. It made me decide to take steps to get my thinking back on track, and I assumed (hoped?!) everything else would follow.

Stuart starts this book with a short statement, "*The smallest change can make the biggest difference*". I didn't jump out of bed every day ready to embrace the world, but I made a small change to my thinking and it was completely empowering. With a clear determination to take a positive approach and concentrate on what I could change, rather than what I couldn't, I began to see new opportunities. I lobbied my employers to let me hire a business coach who gave me the confidence to accept new challenges. I was saying yes to new experiences; ones I would never have had the confidence to accept previously. I began accepting speaking slots at events and decided to use Social Media to help raise my profile in my industry. The positive feedback from industry peers increased my confidence and has led to a new job opportunity.

I also decided my work/life balance was wrong and though I don't get it right every day, I believe I have a healthier approach to working and am now getting more time to focus on family life.

The small change I made to my life didn't take money or resources, I had no excuse NOT to do it! It may seem idealistic to move from concentrating on the negatives in life to the positives, but it works. I'm human and don't get it right all the time, yet the more I make a conscious decision to be happy; the more I decide to focus on the positives in life, the more relaxed and calm I feel. It gives me a concrete foundation on which to tackle the more negative aspects of my life and it is empowering knowing that I can take small steps to make big differences.

Claire

MAY 1st

# Take the opportunity today to write out your relationship goals.

This could be a difficult one for many people. Identifying what we want our relationships to be like takes some serious thought. If we're not careful we'll end up with a wish list that is impossible to fulfil. We run the risk of wishing for relationships where we are always superior, are always in the right, have full control and are basically treated like royalty. And why shouldn't we? (Joking!)

Seriously, we all realise that relationships of any kind take a lot of time, commitment and *work*. All of which we could well do without sometimes but on retrospect appreciate as prerequisite for something deep and meaningful.

So, as you compose your goals list, be careful what you wish *for*.

*" Love is NOT created as a result of conditions, certain conditions are created as a RESULT of love. "* - Neale Donald Walsch

MAY 2nd

# Take the opportunity today to sing out loud - because you can!

There's not much in life more joyful than singing your heart out. Music is ubiquitous because of the sheer joy we get from it. Singing without care of who's listening is like a shout from our soul. It is like a pronouncement that we are alive. Every culture in every country on the planet sings - that can only be because it is a profound expression of who we are. It is primeval, natural and makes you feel goooood! Sing. Sing loudly, and to hell with who hears you. :D

To be honest I do this all the time so I speak from experience. There's a running joke in our house that I'm going to be the next big discovery on Britain's Got Talent! (It definitely won't be for singing though.) :)

# Take the opportunity today to laugh at yourself!

We all have a certain amount of critical self talk going on, I know I do. If I'm clumsy in some way I immediately chastise myself: "You clumsy great oaf!" or words to that effect will be heard by anyone close by. I'm trying to resist that as I know it's reinforcing negative thoughts. Now I try to laugh at my clumsiness instead: "Oh that was incredibly clever, maybe I should stub all of my bare toes on this chair leg and see if I can break a window with the power of sound!"

Something like that will usually make me smile through the pain.

Laughing at yourself for a multitude of things will actually reduce stress and make you an easier person to be around. If you find it difficult, try it first when you're on your own. Once you have mastered turning your frustration into something comical when you're alone you'll be able to do it in company too. Then everyone can have a laugh at your expense.

MAY 4th

# Take the opportunity today to write down 10 things you like about your life.

Whether you think you like your life or not doing this little exercise will reveal some surprises - maybe. You'll get to 6 or 7 with ease but then you might have to think a bit. If you find it really easy, possibly you have some frivolous ones in there; I like my cuddly toy collection for instance. If you got to 10 without a blink of an eye try another 5 or 10. The idea is to 'think' about what you like about your life. The harder you think the more you'll come up with. Do a list of a hundred if you want.

When you've finished, read that list over and over for a few days. Let it sink in just what a great life you already have.

(Maybe you like being a Jedi.)

MAY 5th

# Take the opportunity today to write down 5 things you like about your job.

Most people moan about their job. They wish they could win the lottery so they can quit. They imagine the relief of being able to clear their desk and walk out the door knowing they don't have to come back.

Well, today try to think of just 5 things you '*like*' about your job. Find just 5 positive things. Maybe there are some colleagues there that you like. Maybe the hours are convenient for you. Maybe you enjoy meeting the customers at least. If you put your mind to it I'm sure you can find at least 5 - probably many more. Once you do you will feel differently about your work. It's another way to get in touch with gratitude, the single quickest way to change your feelings about something.

Try it and I bet you'll have a better day at work. :)

MAY 6th

# Take the opportunity today to try something you think you can't do.

How many conversations do you remember where you said that you couldn't do something? You know the ones... 'Oh, I'm terrible at remembering names...' or, 'I'm useless at DIY...' or, 'Maths was never my strong point...' - you get the picture.

These statements aren't so much a statement of fact or truth but rather a statement of what we don't like to do because we find it difficult. It takes too much thinking. Way too much effort. You could say these examples we use are outside of our comfort zone. The thing is, the only way to push ourselves is to do the thing that we find difficult. That's one way in which we can grow. You'll probably find that most of those things aren't so difficult after all - it's just that you've got into the habit of 'not' doing them. Do them, see how rewarding it is to actually be able to fix that shelf or solve that problem or improve that memory. That will then spur you on to have a go at more and more things that previously you thought you couldn't do.

In actual fact there's nothing that you *can't* do, only those things you choose *not* to do.

Go on - you'll surprise yourself.

> Today I bought curtains!. :)

## MAY 7th

# Take the opportunity today to write a list of things you're good at - the longer the better! :)

Most of us find it easy to be critical of the things we think we can't do when in actual fact there's a ton of stuff that we do day in day out that we're good at. Today let's remember all those things. Make the list as long as you can. Put it somewhere you can easily lay your hands on it and the next time you hear yourself (or anyone else) say you can't do something read that list. Keep the positive at the front of your mind, the negative you can work on.

> *" It's the most unhappy people who most fear change. "*
>
> - Mignon McLaughlin

# Take the opportunity today to revisit your old music collection.

If you're like me you still have music on vinyl and tape. If you're under 30 you've probably never had any that wasn't on CD! :)

Whatever medium you have your music stored, trawl back through it and play some tunes from your past. You'll get an immediate trip down memory lane as each memorable song from your past will be connected to some event or experience. Sadly for me I don't even have a record deck or tape player anymore so I'll have to go through my iTunes library and see what I can find there. Failing that I suppose I could always search through my record collection and then see if I can find those tunes on YouTube.

Enjoy! :)

# Take the opportunity today to dance.

Does this need any explaining at all?

This is a primal instinct whether you think you have two left feet or not, dancing is in your genes. Get in touch with your body, put on some loud music and dance!

Some of you might want to Salsa, some might want to Boogie, others might want to headbang! Whichever you prefer is fine, all dance demonstrates who we are. It puts us back in touch with our feelings and our bodies.

It's really good exercise too.

## " *Change brings opportunity.* "

- Nido Quebein

MAY 10th

# Take the opportunity today to step towards one of your relationship goals.

Start with a small step if it'll be easier. Build momentum until you can take bigger, more profound steps. Be aware of how you're feeling as you interact with those you wish to have relationships with. Allow the waxing and waning of the mood to just be what it is. Look to the long term outcome of your words and actions rather than any short term reactions. Have the right intention and persevere.

There is no greater reward in life than the relationships we have with others. The vast majority of us wouldn't want to live the rest of our lives on a desert island - we need company. We need relationships. Being in relationship with others helps us compromise, helps us think outside the box, helps us grow.

Hopefully you have become a better person over the last 10 years. Look back through your memory and you'll see that it was your relationships that made that possible. If you're in a worse place now then think of how your relationships with others played a part in that.

# Take the opportunity today to just be.

Sounds a bit floopy doesn't it? When I say just 'be' I mean just be whatever and whoever you are. Sit in a quiet place and think. Find a hilltop and admire the view. Meditate. Close your eyes and listen to some soothing music. Read. Write your journal. Take a nap.

The point is to be calm and as still as You possibly can. Allow yourself to listen. Either to your thoughts or your breathing or the birds, whatever. It's about You time.

For me, doing nothing helps. So I'll sit and be still for a while or I'll do the hilltop thing. It'll clear your head I promise.

MAY 12th

# Take the opportunity today to take the next step.

If you have ground to a halt with something you are doing in your life, or if you're simply procrastinating, hesitating or otherwise waiting - take the next step. Keep the momentum moving forward.

When you stop for too long inertia sets in and it takes more and more energy to get you going again. A bit like a car's wheels rusting in place if it hasn't moved for too long. Shake the rust off, start your engine, put yourself in gear, check your rear view mirror if you need to then move off. You can move slowly and with caution but move.

*" True life is lived when tiny changes occur. "*

- Leo Tolstoy

# Take the opportunity today to figure out what your distractions are.

Unless you're a robot you will, from time to time, here and there, for one reason or another - get distracted!

We all do.

Now what was I saying? Oh yes... distractions might seem like innocuous strays from the otherwise mundane. They might seem like harmless breaks from monotony. They may even be thought of as part of your creative process. Guess what - they're all of those things. But, when you have a lot of them then you can bet your bottom dollar they are avoidance techniques. Strategies employed to keep you from doing something that '*needs*' to be done. They will speed your clock up and before you know it another week has gone by and 'that thing' still isn't done. It may just mean the lawn didn't get trimmed, or the garage didn't get cleared out or that rubbish didn't get taken to the dump.

Or, it may mean that difficult phone call didn't happen, or that important piece of work was not completed, or... you get the idea.

Be aware of what you are being distracted from - and why. Then remember:- <u>Do what needs to be done, when it needs to be done.</u>

# Take the opportunity today to write your resignation letter! You don't have to deliver it just yet.

You get a good feeling just reading that don't you? Imagine in the nicest way possible you could tell your boss - "Thanks for everything, but I've found something better." Wow, the relief. The excitement.

OK, some of you reading may already be retired or run your own business or are unemployed at the moment. If you're retired and you don't have the financial resources to do what you want whenever you want - imagine that you do. If you run your own business I'm sure you have your fair share of headaches - imagine that you're able to employ someone else to run the day to day side of things freeing up your time to do what you want whenever you want. If you're unemployed - imagine you land a job doing what you love to do and get paid handsomely for it.

The point here is to get in touch with that feeling of freedom, of abundance. Once you get in touch with that feeling you start your subconscious mind running to find a way to make that happen in reality. A super computer working just for You.

Write the letter, be as kind as you can be with your words - we don't want any negative emotions bubbling to the fore here. Make it tangible, readable and enjoyable.

At the very least it'll put a smile on your face!

:)

# Take the opportunity today to step outside your comfort zone.

It's nice to feel safe and secure. To not worry about anything. To not have a care in the world. But, at some point most of us want to grow. We want to achieve and to experience new things and challenge ourselves. Well none of that can happen without stepping outside of your comfort zone. Think of anything worthwhile that has happened in your life and I'll bet you were outside of your comfort zone when it happened. Maybe you were taking an exam, or doing your driving test, or asking someone on a date, or presenting at a meeting, or doing a sponsored event. It's no surprise that once you succeeded in that task you felt elated and energised. It's because you just proved to yourself that you could do that thing that you were worried you couldn't do. You just stepped up. You just grew. It can be an uncomfortable feeling - but it's a great feeling.

## " The key to change... is to let go of fear. "

- Roseanne Cash

MAY 16th
# Take the opportunity today to fail at something.

Whoa! What? You want me to fail at something - on purpose!?

That doesn't make sense.

Actually, I'm not suggesting that you fail on purpose. I'm suggesting that you try something that you'll find really difficult. Something that if you succeeded you'd really grow. Push yourself - hard! A bit like yesterday's guide of stepping outside of your comfort zone today is about taking that to the nth degree.

So what will happen if you fail? You'll be able to draw some inspiration from the fact that you tried, maybe even came close. Learnt what you might be able to do differently next time in order to succeed. Realise that taking risks and raising your head above the parapet drives you forward. If you *only* attempt things that you're pretty sure you can achieve how will you experience something exciting?

Going for it when others are afraid to, or tell you you're not able, enhances your living experience. It will get your adrenalin pumping and it will put a smile on your face - once the grimace has worn off!

The world's leading marketers have a term for failure - they call it testing! So go and test.

But what if you succeed?

Then wow! Now try something else you might fail at.

MAY 17th

# Take the opportunity today to write down 10 things you like about your body.

To be honest I'm not one to dwell on my body shape although there are certain things about my physique that I'd like to improve, and I could certainly be fitter. But for a lot of people the sight of their own naked body fills them with shame. What a shame. This is the only vehicle we get to travel in through this life so let's appreciate it. You may be riding in a Rolls Royce or a clapped out old banger but if it's still getting you from A to B then thank it. Be grateful for it.

From time to time it might break down and need some expert attention but in the meantime spend some time making it as comfortable as possible to travel in, give it what it needs to run as smooth as possible and give it a thorough spring clean every now and then. It's the only one you have so look after it. Imagine for a moment if you knew that your present car was the last you'd have and public transport was being fazed out. Bikes have been banned. That car is your ONLY mode of transport from now on - would you look after it better?

Now stand back and take a good look. If it was your car and you had to think of 10 things you liked you might start with - it's got a good sound system, or at least 3 good tyres, or it's a nice colour, or it handles pretty good. You get the idea, now use that analogy on yourself.

Bob Proctor once said: 'Always be happy with what you have, but never satisfied.' It's insightful because most of us connect the two emotions. Incorrectly! You can be happy with what you've achieved in life so far, but not satisfied you've done enough. You can be happy with your present home but not satisfied with how big it is or where it is. Dissatisfaction drives us to improve, but it shouldn't negate the appreciation for what we have.

# Take the opportunity today to write down 10 things you like about your personality.

Similar to yesterday's guide - this is about building a really positive image of yourself. This is about changing the way you think about yourself. Rather than continually dwelling on what you perceive as negative let's turn that 180 degrees and just start looking at the good things about You.

When you do this you will start to feel more confident not only about who you are but also how you might become who you want to *Be*. Standing still in life is a bit like keeping your savings under the mattress - over time inflation will make them worthless. If you're not moving forward you're falling back.

Give it some time, we're all incredible in our own way. We all have our good points. Identify yours. Recognise what other people find valuable about you. Uncover the real you, the one that wants to live a better life. A happier life. A more fulfilled life.

This exercise will help.

# Take the opportunity today to write down 10 things you like about your relationships.

Remaining in this strategy again - this time describe what it is about the various different relationships you have that you like. Relationships with your loved ones, with your friends, with work colleagues, with the wider community - all of them. As you do this you might start to see a pattern, this in turn might help you identify things that are missing from your relationships that need improvement.

Apart from anything else writing these positive points down will make you feel good, more connected and appreciated.

MAY 20th

# Take the opportunity today to write down 10 things you like about your home.

Don't underestimate this one. Your home is your sanctuary, your comfort, your security, your centre of peace. OK, so you have kids or dogs or BOTH! (So maybe after 10pm it gets peaceful.)

Your home should be the one constant where you can be yourself. With all the many guises we wear in an average day it's good to come home and just be you. So appreciate your home, it may not be your dream home, it may not be arranged the way you'd prefer, it may not contain the kinds of things you long for. But it is your shelter from the storm - at least you have a shelter from the storm.

Make that list and rather than noticing that leaky tap or the socks on the floor, you'll find yourself wandering around taking more notice of the space you have or the feeling of freedom you get.

# Take the opportunity today to write down the goals you have for your home.

We spend on average at least a third of our life IN our homes. Most of us would like to make some improvements in one way or another (I would like to have a bar for instance!!). Our homes are our sanctuaries, our castles, our nests. They are the one place we can truly be who we are so why not make that space your favourite space to be.

Write down how you would like your home to look and feel. If you can't imagine this with your present home do the exercise based on a dream home. Make it real. Write it in present tense ie: My home IS light and airy, I feel relaxed and calm when I walk around my pool, etc. Put a date of when you will have it.

The first step to getting what you want is to describe what it looks like in detail. If you can see it in your mind's eye you have more chance of achieving it.

MAY 22nd

# Take the opportunity today to organise your own Eat In The Street event.

The Eden Project in Cornwall arranges a nationwide call to all to eat in their street with their neighbours as a way to help bring communities together. This is a two week heads up to organise your own Eat In The Street event. Speak to your neighbours, get involved. This is a great opportunity to connect with people that you ordinarily may only say hi to in passing.

You can find out more info on how to organise your event by going to: **www.thebiglunch.com**

I hope you do as I'm sure it'll be a rewarding experience.

NOTE: The event is on the first Sunday of June each year so the actual date changes each time. For instance The Big Lunch in 2012 is on Sunday June 3rd. :)

# Take the opportunity today to say thank you to everyone for everything.

I know we've done something like this already earlier in the year but today is slightly different. Today I suggest you say thank you not only to everyone you come in to contact with but also to everyone you've ever met. You can do some of that literally eg: pick up the phone and say thanks for something. Alternatively, you can just do it in your head. Either way you will feel something. You will feel the gratitude you are putting out there. This gets you into the habit of being grateful and that is powerful. When you are truly feeling grateful your mood changes for the better, your levels of under-standing and empathy increase and you are much more likely to do more good deeds for others.

*" Gratitude is NOT created as a result of conditions, certain conditions are created as a RESULT of gratitude. "*

- Neale Donald Walsch

MAY 24th

# Take the opportunity today to catch up on some sleep if you need to.

*Zzzzzz!*

Recharge those batteries if you're feeling low on energy. We all need a certain amount of sleep and there are countless studies that have been done over the decades that prove we are less functional in all manor of ways when we are tired.

*'I've got too much to do to get more sleep!'* I hear someone shouting and that may be true. But at some point that'll catch up with you, so you're just going to have to find the time. The less sleep you get the less you'll get time and it'll take more and more time to do it. So you are walking in to a dead end.

SLEEP!

# Take the opportunity today to create a win-win situation with a friend.

I don't know about you but there have been occassions in the past where I've dug my heels in over something so that I could win. It often meant that someone else lost. It might have been an argument or debate, it may have been a negotiation at work or over the price of a house or car. Whatever it was, the important thing to me at the time was to win. We don't want to look like suckers or losers or someone that doesn't know what they're talking about right? Hmm.

Well there's another option. Allow the other party to win too. Compromise so that you both get what you want to some extent. Make it clear in a debate that you value the other's opinion or knowledge but that you simply disagree - they don't have to be wrong. When negotiating, plan ahead so that you can accept their final offer that way you get what you expected and they feel like they had the last say. When buying something of high value try to meet the vendor halfway - you'll both feel better for it. Some of this will prove very difficult and some will come easily, all I suggest is that you try.

MAY 26th

# Take the opportunity today to create a win-win situation with a colleague.

Yesterday's guide might have seemed difficult for some and easy for others. For most of us it's reasonably easy to create a win-win situation with our friends but now try it with a colleague. OK, I know that some of your colleagues *are* your friends. Choose one that's more of an acquaintance - just someone you work with, then create that win-win situation with them. Maybe it's someone in accounts that is hassling you for budget figures or the manager of another department that needs some info from you. Find a way for you both to get what you want. Bit more tricky? Bit more thought needed possibly. You'll get a greater sense of achievment from it though.

Good luck.

## 66 *Invest in the process NOT the outcome.* 99

- Srikumar S. Rao Ph.D

# Take the opportunity today to create a win-win situation with a family member.

Yesterday's guide might have been a bit trickier than the day before but this one may be even harder. Yes, family members are usually more conducive to a win-win situation because we know members of our family so well. However, this very intimacy can be the cause of unrest in many households - especially one with teenagers!

So if you fall into that category, dig deep, stay calm and put your most diplomatic foot forward. You're going to need it!

MAY 28th

# Take the opportunity today to create a win-win situation with someone you don't like.

If you haven't already, flick forward a few pages and reassure your-self this is the LAST of these win-win guides! Thank God! I promise the next few days will be easier.

So how do you go about creating a win-win situation with someone that annoys you? Well, that's probably the hardest thing of all. When we don't like someone we automatically set our competitive button to 'max'. Instinctively we want to create a win (for me), lose (for them) situation with hopefully a good portion of humiliation thrown in. But that's not going to help us in the long term is it? No.

By working at creating a win-win situation you are probably going to set their 'suspicion' gauge running at first, but with a bit of authentic reassurance you'll find that most people will end up try-ing to meet you halfway. If you succeed, your relationship with this person will improve no end. Maybe they are a neighbour that com-plains about the noise, or a work colleague that criticises your work regularly, or maybe someone in your football team who's sense of humour you dislike. Whatever the context, give it a try - the rewards could be very surprising. Many have found best friends this way.

## MAY 29th

# Take the opportunity today to pleasantly surprise someone you know.

Oh good - a nice one! How nice is it to surprise someone with a gift, even if it's just a cup of coffee, or offer to help carry some heavy boxes for them, or give them a lift that's out of your way. It feels great doesn't it? It's empowering. You have the power to make someone's day with a gesture, a compliment, a token of your appreciation. How easy and rewarding is that? Pretty soon you'll be wanting to do that all the time and why not - it's great to do and feels good too.

Have fun, be creative with it, just be sure that it really is a 'pleasant' surprise - no jumping out of cupboards on your other half!

:)

MAY 30th

# Take the opportunity today to do something you've been putting off.

Uh-oh! If you're anything like me that could be a mighty long list. From clearing the garage to swapping that duff lightbulb in the cupboard to cleaning the inside of the car to booking that dentist appointment we all put stuff off. Well, tackle one of them today. Make it the easiest one if you want, but do one. You'll be proud of yourself afterwards.

I decided to look at the Kindle phenomena today. Not from a buyer's point of view but from an author's point of view. Being a technophobe I had convinced myself that it would be really complicated to upload a book I'd written. I presumed that it would need special formatting that I'd struggle with. Today I decided to just have a go. And guess what, it wasn't so bad. Yeah, some of it was misleading and confusing but I got through it and managed to load up a test book I had written a while back. I got my other half to purchase it so I could see how it came out and presto - it's ok. Bring on the next challenge. :)

MAY 31st

# Take the opportunity today to review the guides of this month to see which ones you may have missed.

Oh yes, another month has flown by and I have to say I've missed quite a few of these guides myself this month. Bad author!

I'll have to make a concerted effort to scroll back through them and pick at least one that I can implement asap. If there's a grey box below it means I succeeded.

Remember, if you don't try at least some of these guides nothing in your life will change. Give yourself the best opportunity to change by doing things you don't normally do.

---

Make a note in your journal or diary of any changes
you have noticed since you started this book.

---

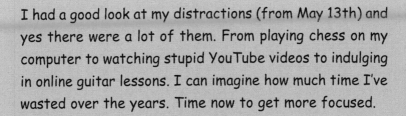

I had a good look at my distractions (from May 13th) and yes there were a lot of them. From playing chess on my computer to watching stupid YouTube videos to indulging in online guitar lessons. I can imagine how much time I've wasted over the years. Time now to get more focused.

# Take the opportunity today to do something that fills you with nostalgia.

Call an old friend or better still go have a coffee with them. Reminisce a while, remember old friends and experiences you shared.

Or, maybe read some of your old love letters. It's ok if you get a little melancholy - it's good to remember. Indulge.

This is a great way to get back in touch with occassions that filled you with good feelings Remember *how* to have those feelings. Sometimes we get so busy we forget.

*" We all have big changes in our lives that are more or less a second chance. "*

- Harrison Ford

JUNE 2nd

# Take the opportunity today to be less judgemental.

*"If you judge someone, you have no time to love them."*

Mother Theresa said that and she was right. When we judge we are at least partially seeing our own faults in others. Because we recognise them in ourselves and dislike them we feel the need to dislike them in others. If only we could forgive our own failings we could forgive them in others. After all none of us are perfect. Jesus said *'Let he who has no sin caste the first stone.'* Coming to the same point.

So the next time you find yourself criticizing someone take a moment to consider if you yourself have acted or thought in a similar way in the past. If you have, ask yourself how you would have liked people to think of you. We have all made mistakes and we'll all make more - let's not condemn each other for them. Show some empathy, some understanding and leave the judge in the courtroom where they belong.

## JUNE 3rd
# Take the opportunity today to eat stuff you shouldn't! :)

Yum!

Come on - you can't diet every day. Life is for living. If you are just starting a diet however you may want to skip this one so you don't lose your momentum. For the rest of you - have a cake!

:)

> **" No one is in control of your happiness but you; therefore, you have the power to change anything about yourself or your life that you want to change. "**
>
> - Barbara de Angelis

OK - so now I feel sick! Enjoyed every bite but I'm glad that only happens once in a while. :)

# Take the opportunity today to see things for what they really are.

You know what I mean right? Sure you do. I could sit here and write a page of words that show you what they are but I'd only be scratching the surface wouldn't I?

We've all got stuff going on that we *say* is this or that. But we know it's not. I mean it could look that way to the untrained eye, to the casual observer, but *we know* it's just a façade for what's really going on.

Take a good look at it today, be as honest with yourself as you can. Allow the discomfort or maybe even pain of looking at it to come through. Welcome it. Once we open the cupboard door and shine a light in there we can see there was nothing to be afraid of.

I know this'll be hard for a lot of people - me included, so lets all dig deep and give it a try. If you've stayed with me this far I know you have the courage to do this.

JUNE 5th

# Take the opportunity today to eat in the street.

The Eden Project in Cornwall arranges a nationwide call to all, to eat in their street with their neighbours as a way to help bring communities together. If this is a Sunday then today's the day - enjoy, laugh, listen, understand, involve, eat, drink, dance and most of all connect.

Remember: the first Sunday in June is on a different date each year so you may have already done this. Having said that, do it again if you want - maybe just your own family!

:D

# Take the opportunity today to donate to a charity you have never donated to before.

You may already donate to a charity or even many charities. If you do you probably know a thing or two about them and what they do. Today, find a bit out about another one. Donate to them. We never know when we might be in need of someone elses charity so let's build up a good deposit in advance. We also don't know what kind of charity we might need in the future so it's good to spread the love as it were. I once spoke to an acquiantance who helped to run a charity and his advice was to stick with one and allow them to know that you are committed to them long term as they can plan more effectively that way. That's good advice and I agree with it. However, it doesn't stop us doing some ad hoc charity donating along side.

JUNE 7th

# Take the opportunity today to check in on an elderly neighbour.

If you have an elderly neighbour it's possible that you already do check in on them. Often though they can go unnoticed as they tend to stay in most of the time. If this is the case, show a friendly face and make sure they are coping ok. We all want our independence so some elderly people can become defensive if you bring that into question. For the most part though I think people appreciate the thought if they are asked if they need anything - I certainly do if I'm unwell and a neighbour asks if they can get anything for me from the shop to save me venturing out.

Worst case scenario; you get a curt reply. Best case scenario; you make a fascinating friend.

> " Loneliness is NOT created as a result of conditions, certain conditions are created as a RESULT of loneliness. "
>
> - Neale Donald Walsch

## JUNE 8th

# Take the opportunity today to give some flowers to a loved one.

This can be done by men OR women. When was the last time you received flowers? Have you ever had flowers arrive for you? If you have you know how great it feels. Pass that feeling on.

If you can't afford to buy flowers go out and pick some (from somewhere that you're allowed) - then deliver them yourself. Enjoy the reaction they get.

JUNE 9th

# Take the opportunity today to do something memorable.

We can all remember certain events in our lives no matter how old we get. The ones that stick with us are because they were so meaningful or fun or exciting. The reason they stay with us is they carry significance. They mean something to us deep down inside. Make one of these memories today. Do something that you'll remember for the rest of your life. It can be big or small, it can involve others or just yourself.

When you think about it, life is just a series of memories, they define who we are to some extent and without them we become lost. Sometimes it takes another person to bring up one of their memories for me to remember it too. That's what happens when you have plenty.

Add another to your memory filing cabinet today.

I went to a property networking meeting and met some interesting people. Everyone was friendly and some I may stay in touch with. Who knows - it could turn out to be a memorable evening.

## JUNE 10th

# Take the opportunity today to think before you speak.

I bet every one of us can remember something that came out of our mouth that we wished we could cram back in. Too late! Once you've said it, it's said. Let's do more listening and contemplating and maybe, just maybe that'll happen less. We can keep our great big size nines out of our mouth.

Do that today and you may very well be glad you did tomorrow.

Being one that always wants to be right I have found myself NOT doing this a lot in the past. It's painful - for both parties. I will make a concerted effort to keep my mouth shut long enough to ponder the reaction of the words running around inside my head before I let them out. Like excited children they need to be calmed before being let out in the street to play. Who knows what kind of mischief they'll get up to if you let them run out unattended?

JUNE 11th

# Take the opportunity today to take a step towards one of your goals for your home.

If you managed to write your list of goals down a couple of weeks ago (May 21st) today is the day to take a step towards one of them. Start looking at homes in the area you want to live on the internet if you aren't in your dream home right now. If you are, go to the store and get those samples of wallpaper you love, create a mood board of colours and patterns or start creating a budget for the refurbishments you wish to make. Get some home design magazines and start cutting out pictures of how you'd like your dream home to look and feel. Do something, anything, that starts the ball rolling. If you never start you'll never finish!

I regularly do the looking on the internet thing. I'm convinced that if I look then I'll find. If I keep thinking 'I can't afford it yet' then I'll never discover that bargain or that dream location that I desire. Em does the magazine looking, she loves to collect beautiful images of interiors etc. Both of us like to hunt around in reclaim yards too - knowing full well we have nowhere to put anything if we bought it. Still, we're honing exactly what we like so when the time comes we'll know right where to go to get what we want.

# Take the opportunity today to encourage someone.

Can you remember a time that someone encouraged You to do something? Remember how it made you feel? Probably you felt pretty good about it. I'm sure it gave you a lift and the motivation to continue with whatever it was that you were trying to achieve.

Give someone else that feeling. You never know where it might lead them. A little encouragement is sometimes all we need to do something daring or amazing.

*" The man who looks for security, even in the mind, is like a man who would chop off his limbs in order to have artificial ones which will give him no pain or trouble. "*

- Henry Miller

# Take the opportunity today to have fun. You remember how don't you? ;)

All work and no play makes Jack a dull boy, right?

We've all heard that saying haven't we? And we all relate to it. If we don't recharge the batteries with enough rest AND play we can quickly become exhausted. Play actually energises us. Our happy hormones get triggered along with adrenalin and we feel able to carry on with playful activities far longer than non-playful ones that require the same effort.

Besides anything else life is supposed to be *fun*. If you can somehow have more fun even when you're working then even better. Think about all the leisure activities there are in the world - it's because we are programmed to seek out and have fun!

Make sure something you do today involves really enjoying yourself.

# Take the opportunity today to start over afresh. The past has gone - let it go!

At the risk of sounding pop psych - you can't live in the past. It's unchangeable. You can't influence anything that's 'already' happened. This is obvious, right? It's so easy though to rerun old tapes in our minds of events that have hurt us, offended us, traumatised us. It's a way of justifying our feelings. We use it to convince ourselves that someone else is to blame for...whatever! We convince ourselves that we are scarred by those events - defined maybe by them. But we're not! It's a choice. We can choose not to be scarred by them. Yeah it takes quite a bit of effort depending on how hurt you believe you were. I'm not suggesting that your pain at the time wasn't valid - I'm sure it was 100%. But that was then and this is NOW!

Let it go.

Accept what happened. Accept how it made you feel at the time. Then - let it go.

If you want a brighter future step out of the darkness of the past.

JUNE 15th

# Take the opportunity today to pamper someone close to you.

You know how great it feels when someone really spoils you. Usually on your birthday! You get the breakfast you want, you can lounge around if you want - being waited on. Maybe you're treated to dinner at a nice restaurant or given a lovely relaxing massage. It feels great because we feel valued and loved. So, pass that on. Don't wait for someone's birthday, do it today. Then, when you realise how good it makes you feel, do it often. :)

You never know - you might be repaid with the same.

I had intended to give my other half a massage today as she had spent the day in London working. The 5am start and 8pm homecoming meant she would be totally bombed. As it turned out, after I had made her dinner and put a glass of red wine in her hand she wanted nothing more than a foot rub. So, a foot rub she got - and that was fine because it meant we got to sit together for half an hour uninterrupted by dogs wanting to jump up. This was half hour just for us. With the best intentions we don't do it often. I now know how to get her to myself - foot rub! :)

# Take the opportunity today to ask for help.

OK put your hand up if you find asking for help difficult. Yes, I have my own hand up right now - literally, I stopped typing and put my hand up!

Why?

Why do we find that difficult? Maybe because it reinforces that we can't do this task by ourselves and we feel we should. Maybe we feel that it would impose on others to ask for help. Maybe we think we can't afford the help that we require.

Let's answer those 'maybes' one at a time:

1) The idea we should be able to do everything by ourselves is simply ridiculous. Would you expect it of anyone else? Would you ask your window cleaner to rewire your house? It's ok to NOT be able to do everything, we all have different strengths. It's ok to ask for help with something you know you *can* do on your own because some-days we just need a bit of help.

2) I read somewhere recently that if you want someone to like you, rather than do them a small favour, get them to do *you* one. Yes, we like to help others because it reinforces our natural desire to be wanted and valued. When you ask for help you're actually giving a gift to the other person. (I know - some people don't see it that way so don't ask *them!*)

3) What's your time worth to you? Sometimes you might have to buy someone else's time to get something done properly; on time; or without going insane! Understand the cost of not paying some-one else.

JUNE 17th

# Take the opportunity today to take your time.

"I haven't got time to take my time!" I can hear some of you thinking. Well, that may seem accurate - but is it?

How often have you made mistakes because you rushed something, then had to spend even more time to put things right? My guess is at least a few times. So, yes, you may be up against it most of the time but try to slow down here and there. As the saying goes: More speed, less haste.

This is not a flippant request for you to get lethargic or lazy or to waste time. This is about taking the time to allow yourself to absorb what's going on. Sometimes we are so focused on the deadline we can't see the better, easier solution right in front of us.

Try it, it may work out really well for you.

I wrote this guide this morning then went off to sort some business out. It wasn't urgent but I was adhering to my own advice of do what needs to be done as soon as possible. So I got finished where I was and had to move on to another town to sort something else out - again, not urgent but I thought I might as well do it asap. Then I changed my mind as I remembered the guide of today. Instead I decided to go to the cafe and grab a cuppa and a read of my magazine. I got talking to the new owner of the cafe and before I knew it I was sorting out some potential new business with him. You never know how or when serendipity is going to show up in your life. :)

# Take the opportunity today to focus on one thing at a time.

One of the terrible ailments I suffer from is 'distractionitis'. Sounds bad doesn't it? I'm like a magpie in a tinfoil factory, I flit from this thing to that thing to that other thing and back again. It's a miracle I managed to create the habit to write this book every day.

I am as I write this, going through Bob Proctor's Goal Achiever's Program and the biggest piece of advice my facilitator has given me is 'focus'. Keep on with one thing until it's done. That was hard to hear. I've been like this for 46 years! I'm an artist for goodness sake - I need my freedom of expression. Blah blah! The thing is I know that he's right. I can get a lot of things done at once - I'm a natural multi-tasker. But, if I want to get something done really well I need to stop flitting around and just focus on *that thing* until it's completed.

This doesn't mean you can't get anything else done. Hey, we've all got to pay the bills. The point is, if you have something that either needs to be done or you really desire it to be done, then focus on that thing as much as you can and allow all the other unimportant distractions (TV, the pub, surfing the net, etc.) to take a back seat for a while. You'll be amazed at how productive you become.

JUNE 19th

# Take the opportunity today to give yourself a little gift.
# Go on, you deserve it. :)

Hopefully you have several goals lists by now and you're working your way towards achieving them. As you reach the little milestones along the way remember to keep rewarding yourself. As Anthony Robbins explains we need to make new neural links of pleasure to our new behaviour and habits in order to solidify them. As we associate good things with our achievements we give oursleves renewed energy to reach the next one.

Give yourself a reward today even if it's just a self pat on the back - you deserve it!

## " Change in all things is sweet. "

- Aristotle

# Take the opportunity today to help a work colleague you don't particularly like.

I have found in the past that by helping someone I didn't particularly like or get along with in the work place was often reciprocated more readily than when I helped those that were more like friends.

I think this was because the people we get along with just expect to be helped when needed as you would expect to be helped by them. But when you help that someone that rubs you up the wrong way they notice it more. They don't expect you to help them so when you do it really stands out for them. They then seem to search for the opportunity to repay that help. Maybe some part of them doesn't want to 'owe' you. But who cares right? Just help them and let them deal with their own thoughts about your motives.

Oh and by the way - don't expect to get help in return, just do it to be helpful. Your work relationships will improve no end.

JUNE 21st

# Take the opportunity today to listen to your inner voice.

Have you ever wondered 'who' owns that inner voice? You know the one. The one that says: 'You know what, I don't think you can do that.' or it might be the one that says: 'Yes, that's what I should do.' Either way that's your inner voice. If you find you're in disagreement with that inner voice ask yourself - 'Who is that anyway?'

Who is it that you're arguing with?

It can only be you right? So what part of you is saying something contrary to what YOU are thinking? If it's being negative then it's your fear personality. If it's being positive then it's your passion personality. Ask yourself who you'd rather listen to - your fear or your passion.

Stop for a moment and listen to your passion personality, if your fear personality raises it's voice just ask it to wait it's turn. Listen carefully to what your passion personality is saying. That way lies joy.

*For most people there are no inner voices spurring them on with encouragement.*

*- Richard Bandler*

JUNE 22nd

# Take the opportunity today to laugh out loud - go find something you like to laugh at!

Laughter is one of humanities greatest gifts. We can't tell if any other species laugh. We suspect some do. Dog owners will try and convince you their dog smiles and sometimes even laughs. Scientists studying primates will try and convince you that within their social structure they laugh. But for the moment we only know for sure that we do.

So, go and find an old joke book or an old film or a new one for that matter, or read some cartoons or just spend some time with a friend that always makes you howl - and spend some time laughing. It's good for the soul. It's great for relieving stress. It releases happy hormones in to your system and it makes you feel great.

Spend more time laughing!

As I finished writing that last sentence my other half walked in with a cup of tea for me - she read the page then said: "I laugh in your face every day!" I replied "You laugh in my face but I laugh *at* your face!" We then had a good laugh. (When I say 'we' I mean ME - she just wanted to tip the tea on my head!)

JUNE 23rd

# Take the opportunity today to sort through your old clothes and donate those which you really don't wear anymore. You know you want to.

If you're like me there are clothes at the bottom of the draw that you haven't even looked at in the last 12 months let alone worn. Find time today to rearrange those to the top so they get worn. While you're at it get rid of some items you've grown tired of wearing, don't fit anymore or you just don't want now. There are plenty of charity shops thankful for donations - even if the clothes are in disrepair most will take as rags (as long as they're all clean).

You'll feel better for having done some decluttering and you'll find some nice clothes you'd simply forgotten about.

When I do this from time to time I sometimes find gifts that I've never worn or maybe only worn once. That makes me feel really guilty so I'm grateful for the chance to make use of something somebody took time effort and money to get for me.

# Take the opportunity today to make amends.

Have you ever upset somebody and never apologised? Even if you don't agree that what you did or said was wrong or incorrect? Even when you now know that they are getting upset and that is their responsibility, that what you say or do should have no bearing on how they 'feel'?

If so, make amends.

Life is too short to hold grudges or to have grudges held against us. Make amends with that person even if they are no longer a part of your life. Find some way to patch it up, make it good. I'm not suggesting you admit you were wrong if you think you weren't, I'm just saying find a way to make it better.

Then you can take a deep breath and carry on with your life - you'll feel better I promise.

JUNE 25th

# Take the opportunity today to exercise.

Exercise! It needs no explanation does it? Most of us need to exercise more, me included, if we want this body of ours to last well in to the future. You notice I used the word 'well'. We not only want to last a long time but we want to retain our health for as long as possible too.

Start today with just some regular light stretching. Maybe trot up and down the stairs a few times to get your heart going. Exercise itself makes us feel better so it's a good habit to start.

Those of you who do exercise regularly, see if you can encourage a friend to do the same.

A few weeks ago I promised myself I would stretch for 15 minutes each and every day. I think I lasted two days maybe three. Hmm! So today I get another chance to make that happen - I'm going to do it right now, literally right now after this full stop. I encourage you to do the same.

# Take the opportunity today to think differently about something.

We can, on occasion, every now and again get attached to some of the thoughts we have. You know the ones; my neighbour is really annoying because... Or; people that read such and such a paper are... Or; those people claiming benefits when they don't even bother to find work and look after themselves are...

Most of us have thoughts like that.

Now choose one of those thoughts, one that you know very well, and just as an exercise imagine it's wrong. Place yourself in a situation where the truth about something is the opposite of that thought you usually have. For example, your neighbour may be doing their best from where they are and it's You that *chooses* to become annoyed because of your lack of understanding about *their* circumstances. Imagine you are having an incredibly traumatic time at the moment, so much so that You behave in a way similar to your neighbour and it's your neighbour thinking that You are annoying.

Think about that today - just as an exercise.

# Take the opportunity today to turn the other cheek.

Our ego more often than not rules a large part of our conscious lives. It gets us in to a lot of trouble. It's constantly on the look out for confirmation of our paradigms and belief systems. This can manifest in many ways, most are harmless, but some can be very confrontational. Imagine you're a gang member in a ghetto somewhere and somebody you don't know looks at you from across the street for a second or two. It could be because they think they know you, or they like your T-shirt, or they're thinking of asking you for directions. You may interpret that gaze as an afront. You may think it's a gesture of disrespect. Your ego kicks in and whispers in your inner ear *'That guy is trying to intimidate you, right in your own neighbourhood.'* That thought may lead on to you strutting across the street to confront the guy, and so on etc. We know how that's going to end.

Well that's an extreme example I know, but now think how you may be doing that from time to time in a much subtler way. Screaming at someone who just cut you up on the road, or giving someone a dirty look because they bumped into you on the street without saying exceuse me, or becoming annoyed that 'someone' used the last of the milk and now there's none left for you to have a cup of tea.

Next time something like that happens, just turn the other cheek. Forgive them. Let it go. Maybe the car driver is trying desperately to get to hospital - no excuse I know but if it were you, you might be rushing a bit right? Maybe the person that bumped into you was so focused on the upset of just being fired they didn't notice the collission. Maybe, the last of the milk is being replaced right at that second - you can wait two minutes can't you?

It takes a bit of practise but try it next time one of those thoughts comes into your mind. And remember; your ego can be your worst side as well as your best side. Give the best side more exposure to the outside world. :)

*" Faced with the choice between changing one's mind and proving that there is no need to do so, almost everyone gets busy on the proof. "*

- John Kenneth Galbraith

# Take the opportunity today to be non-judgemental.

Now that's a hard one!

Hmm, where to start? I suppose the easiest way to have a go at this is to first *be* judgemental. Then, after your initial thoughts about something or someone give yourself the opportunity to look at it from a different angle. Our present belief systems are so ingrained it would be almost impossible to just stop being judgemental, so allow it. Accept it. Then question it.

Then you might find yourself being judgemental about your judgementalism.

As I said - it's a hard one, but have a go anyway.

# Take the opportunity today to give someone your undivided attention for as long as they need it.

We all want to be heard, it's part of our social DNA. We are pack creatures and good communication is vital to our very survival. But these days it seems that listening and hearing are two different things.

Have you ever had a conversation with someone and you just know that they are just waiting for their turn to speak? Not too satisfying is it? Next time you're in a conversation be aware if *you* are actually listening or just waiting for the chance for *you* to speak. The simplest way to give your undivided attention is to not think about saying anything. Just listen, and when it naturally becomes your turn - if you're asked for your opinion for instance, then ask something relevant to what you've just heard which will allow the other to continue explaining.

When this becomes a habit you'll not only get a lot more out of your conversations, because you will have really understood the other's point of view, but you'll find that other people, through the law of reciprocation, will listen more intently to you. This leads to deeper communication, increased levels of empathy and understanding and better relationships all round.

JUNE 30th

# Take the opportunity today to review the guides of this month to see which ones you may have missed.

I hope you find these reminder pages at the ends of the months as useful as I do. I take a breath of relief knowing that I can go back and try something I missed first time around. It's odd that timing is so important in these tasks. Something I didn't try on the day it came up may jump out at me as I re-read them, almost as if I wasn't supposed to implement it back then - that *now* is the perfect time to try something. One of my pet sayings is 'Timing is always Perfect' and I really believe that. Not in a fatalistic way, not in a *it must be destiny* way, but rather, in a *your subconscious knows what's best for you and when* way.

Maybe that sounds a bit floopy. Anyway, I find it useful to always believe something is happening at that particular time because that's the best time for it to be happening.

---

Make a note in your journal or diary of any changes you have noticed since you started this book.

---

CASE STUDY 3

# Tina's Story

A few years ago I had a bad relationship with my father, mainly due to me wanting to be free and my dad wanting me to stay put. This led to me living my life *how* I wanted and *as* I wanted. In a way I was running away and making myself find my own path in life.

I started to date a guy called Shannon, a West Indian man which was a secret from my parents. Coming from an Asian/Indian background, there were certain traditions my father would prefer me to live by, dating someone of the same background etc. - but I did the opposite. Not purposely, but I thought it's what I genuinely wanted. I really thought this man, who was a friend, was what I wanted.

My relationship with my dad remained bad, we used to avoid each other in the same house, eat at different times etc. and this used to cause tension amongst the whole family. Eventually I moved out and moved in with Shannon without telling my parents. A few days later I finally told them, my dad asked me to pick my clothes up and drop the house keys off. I did and continued living with my boyfriend.

My parents finally accepted him after I was involved in a car crash, but then I realised, it was not what *I* wanted. I didn't want to be with someone like my boyfriend and live the way I did - a laid back lifestyle with no goals, plus he had debts and financial problems but took no action to better himself. So I ended it with him after 2 years of dating, coincidently at the same time as things got better with my dad.

I moved back home and things were really good - family dinners, chats, just a really good family atmosphere. They were happy to have me back but it was slightly uncomfortable at first. I think that was me feeling the guilt for leaving home and being with someone who wasn't right for me etc.

Months later I met Tom, again a secret, as he was a West Indian guy too, but a lot different than Shannon and more of what I thought I wanted. Security, loving, attentive, the feel good factor, supportive etc. But again after 2 years of dating, I realised he *wasn't* what I wanted either, he was too laid back, aiming to be an actor but not committing to it, living with his mum and not saving to move out. I ended it with Tom and stayed single for a couple of months.

In that time I became a lot clearer about what I wanted. I wanted someone who was strong, hard working, had goals, was encouraging, who planned for the future, who wanted to settle down and raise a family. Someone that had the same background as me so we could share the same morals, same language, so we could raise children with a common culture etc.

I bought a house so felt secure in myself and my future, my dad supported me in this so I felt really protected too.

It was then I reunited with a guy I had met at the gym some years back, an Indian guy. He had everything I wanted - his own business, he was hard working, secure, disciplined, had life goals, ambitions, he was ready to settle down and wanted children etc. Within 6 months we got engaged, we found out that our fathers studied together at school in East Africa and that we have some mutual families, so everything felt so familiar and right.

It was refreshing having my parents know about my relationship - it was like I was doing the right thing and had nothing to hide. Six months later we got married and I'm living the life I dreamed of.

Looking back on my journey I can see that my father played a big role in my life, he was my backbone and without that I was searching for a replacement and therefore dating guys who would give me love, care and attention but not the other important things I valued.

I also realised that by being true to myself, I can make my dream come true only if I take control and make it happen. I took control, created the change I wanted and am now living the change I dreamed of.

I feel secure, calm, at peace and ease within me and with our families.


Tina

# Take the opportunity today to feel the sun on your face.

If you're in the UK then you know how difficult that is. Probably the only worse place to feel the sun on your face is Wales! Either way you'll understand immediately why feeling the sun on your face is so therapeutic. Not only are you triggering your own internal Vitamin D production but you just get such a feeling of well being. I feel energised but relaxed in the same moment. I like to stand in my garden, eyes closed, facing the sun just breathing deeply.

What a great feeling.

You'll notice I put this one at the beginning of July to give those in the UK (and Wales) the best possible chance of actually doing this TODAY!

Still, it's only a 50/50 chance, right?

;)

It was actually sunny this morning (when I got up anyway) so I got to spend 5 minutes in my garden doing this. It really got the day off to a good start. Mmm, and... relax!

JULY 2nd
# Take the opportunity today to stop believing everything you think.

By Dr Mark Atkinson as read on Finerminds blog:

'One of the most common causes of unhappiness is living in your head and taking seriously the 'stories' that your head creates. Most of what we think isn't true and has no bearing on reality. One of the quickest ways to experience True Happiness is to shift from being identified with our thoughts to being the awareness *of* our thoughts. A simple and quick way to disengage any stressful story that your head is making up is to notice what the stressful thought is, for example 'there's no way I can get this done in time'– then say that stressful thought out loud (or silently in your head) very slowly – with a few seconds gap in between each word. Breathe slowly throughout and repeat 2 to 3 times, noticing as you do so how a sense of inner spaciousness, well-being and balance starts to open up inside of you. This is the experience of what I call the true Self, the source of true happiness! If you practice this often throughout the day for three days I am almost certain you will experience a profound shift in the way you feel. You can also use this technique for freeing yourself from any self-limiting beliefs that you have.'

To learn more about the great work Finerminds is doing visit: **www.finerminds.com** - they've always got great and inspirational content there.

JULY 3rd
# Take the opportunity today
# to start over.

You know what it is you need to start over. Think about it for a while and it will become apparent. Let it go and start over. It's not quitting, it's not letting it get the better of you. It's giving yourself the chance to move on, start anew.

'A change is as good as a rest', they say.

'There's no point flogging a dead horse', is another one.

Sometimes you have to realise when something has has come to it's natural end, spending more time on it really is a *waste* of time. It's hard to move on I know, I'm definitely one for trying to make something work but sometimes it's like giving the kiss of life to Tutankhamun's mummy - it's pointless.

It could be a project you've been working on, it could be your job, it could be your relationship or one you're trying to get in to. Think about it today and consider if it's a waste of time, consider whether it's time to start over.

JULY 4th

# Take the opportunity today to Be Independent.

This is a big day for all those in the US obviously but Being independent means more than being separate. The US celebrations are based on becoming free from the tyranny of the British Empire but what does being independent mean on an individual scale?

For me, this means taking responsiblity for myself, my actions, my welfare and every other aspect of my life. That doesn't mean I don't want an ambulance to turn up if I need it, or the police to come to my rescue if I'm being mugged - I pay taxes to ensure those are available when I need them. But I try not to put myself in harm's way from injury or violation - and that's *my* responsibility.

Independence also means making my own way in life too, I work for myself now but when I worked for someone else I never felt like I was *owed* a job, I knew I had to *earn* it. I knew if I made a mistake or didn't have the skills that I would suffer the consequences. So, I always made sure I overdelivered, improved my skills by continually learning and was always very conscientious. Because of that commitment I've never been fired.

Being independent is not *always* possible. If you are in any way impaired to such an extent that you need help from others to either get around or look after yourself or earn money you can still be independent of thought. All too often we lean on people emotionally, usually those closest to us, to fulfil some need *we* have. This comes from a sense of lack. Even when you need somebody to help you, you don't need *that* somebody to help you. You could get that help from somebody else. As soon as you make someone else responsible for *your* feelings about something you have relinquished being independent.

We are not always responsible for the things that happen to us, but we are responsible for how we react to those things.

Consider today in what ways you may not be taking full responsibility and therefore not *being* independent.

# Take the opportunity today to have a debate about something you believe in.

I love having a debate. Not an argument! A debate. An argument is based on only trying to get your point across without considering what the other party is saying. Debating however, can really get your mental juices flowing. If you debate with someone who has an alternate belief even better - if you get your ego out of the way you may even *change* your belief to theirs. The process of debating will also improve your articulation skills which will bring you confidence and clarity. Democracy is built on the process of debate. You will hone your skill of persuasion, logic and wit in the process which will serve you well in all other aspects of life.

Remember all good debate is good natured - it may get heated but everyone should still be friends afterwards - not the case in most arguments. It's good fun and educational so go flex your debate muscle.

JULY 6th

# Take the opportunity today
# to review your goals.

Throughout this book you have and will continue to come across advice to write and review your goals. Nearly all successful people have goals written down and there's a good reason for it. As previously mentioned, writing them down is the first step to realising them. Taking action is the second and reviewing them is the third.

By reviewing your goals you get to remind yourself that you *have* goals in the first place, determine if you are on the right track to achieving any and allow your subconscious to explore the *hows* of taking steps towards them.

Review them today.

I review my main career goals daily by reading them every morning when I get up and every evening before I go to bed. This keeps them in the forefront of my subconscious and although I can't prove it, it helps keep me focused and motivated to keep those baby steps happening.

# Take the opportunity today to consider your death bed speech.

Sounds a bit morbid doesn't it? It's not supposed to be. Imagine for a moment that you are on your death bed, not some day way off in the future, but next week!

Your family and friends are gathered around the bed and you decide to review your life. You thank them all for being loving friends and family. You thank them for all the wonderful experiences they have shared with you. You then consider if you have any regrets about things you never got around to doing - 99% of us have them.

If you knew you were going to die within a few hours or days and that those things would be left undone, unachieved - how would you feel?

For me, I'd be pretty frustrated that I'd run out of time. I'd probably lie there and ponder those missed opportunities and wonder why I didn't just get on and do them. Life is so short, I'd think, why didn't I just do them?

So that's the point of today's ponder - not to get morbid, but rather to get motivated. Remember those things you keep saying you'd love to do - and start planning them. Today!

Life IS too short. As Buddha once said:

'The trouble is, you think you have time.'

# Take the opportunity today to break a task down into smaller steps.

If you have some tasks on your 'To Do' list that always seem to be moved over onto the next list then the next because you keep putting them off, chances are it's too big to tackle in one go. Take another look at it and see if it can be broken down into smaller chunks that are more manageable. If you can break it down into five steps and you just do one step each day it'll be done in a week.

The best way to get things done and achieve the things you want is to just *Do Them*! So even if you have to break something down into 20 steps - do it and it'll get done.

When you write a book for example there's a lot to think about; the content, the chapters, the introduction, the pitch to a publisher, the marketing plan etc. It can't all be done at the same time so you have to start with writing the first page. Putting stuff in order can be done as you go and that's often the case with many tasks. Breaking the task down is itself the first step to getting it done so pat yourself on the back when you get that part completed.

JULY 9th

# Take the opportunity today to fix something around your home.

Boring!

Yep, I one of those who would rather do just about anything else other than fixing stuff. Partly because over the years I've convinced myself I'm useless at that sort of thing but mainly because it doesn't interest me.

Here's the thing though, as I've got older I've just knuckled down and done it (after much cajoling I hasten to add), and once I do it not only do I find that I'm actually not bad at some things but I get a great sense of pride afterwards. I dislike the process still as I'm likely to cut three bits of wood wrong before I cut the last bit correctly but, if I give myself a break and just plod on regardless I can find it quite rewarding.

If you're the type that likes a bit of DIY then this won't be much of a challenge so maybe go and help someone else fix something at their house. (Hey, come round mine if you like - there'll be plenty to do here!)

JULY 10th

# Take the opportunity today to set someone up to succeed.

Anyone that's done dog training will recognise this technique. The idea is you make a task really easy for a dog to get right so that they get a reward. If repeated over and over the dog will associate the task with the treat. Dogs don't talk human and tend to get frustrated quickly if they don't understand what you're asking them to do - so you make it *easy*.

The same technique can be used with people, not in a condesending way but in a positive affirming way. When teaching a new colleague a company process for instance have it typed out then show them the process so they can see what's expected. If teaching a child, break the task down into the most manageable steps so they keep getting it right whilst continually moving forward. This gives them a sense of achievment and they're much more likely to respond well and feel good.

In every situation today keep thinking how you can get someone to succeed in what they're doing.

---

I had a random thought today about teaching football players to take penalties - start them off with no goal keeper. Start them off by kicking the ball softly so it definitely goes IN. This is setting them up to succeed right from the start. As they get more accomplished the pressure can be ratcheted up until they are facing a goal keeper in a realistic fashion.

---

JULY 11th

# Take the opportunity today to rearrange the furniture in one room.

You never know when a change of scenery will change your mood. After all, it's one of the reasons we go somewhere else for our holiday. We need to get away from the same old same old. Well maybe you don't have the time or the money at the moment to go on holiday but what you do have is the ability to just change the scenery around at home.

Try it - just one room and see how it makes you feel. Whenever I do this I feel re-energised for some reason. I get to re-enjoy the space I'm living in. Plus, it reinforces that I can change how I feel by taking some action. You feel more in control.

(And you'll end up finding that missing remote control, a ball of fluff you could stuff a cushion with and approximately £2.75 in change!!)

:)

# Take the opportunity today to treat others as you'd like to be treated in their position.

I think this comes from the Surmon on the Mount and is just about the only rule we need to live by. If we just acted like this on every occasion, in every situation with everyone we met, the world would be conflict free. It's hard to do though. People get on our nerves sometimes. Hmm.

Unless you're perfect you probably get on someone else's nerves sometimes. Imagine that for a moment, *you* get on someone's nerves. They gripe about you to other people, they may even moan at you to your face. Does that bother you in any way? If it doesn't then move on to the next page, but if it does consider this: you're not doing it on purpose are you? No, so you have your reasons for behaving in the way that gets on someone else's nerves. Guess what? The people that get on your nerves also have *their* reasons.

So the next time you're getting irritated by someone try and understand their reasons, see it from their shoes, imagine you *are* them.

You may just find yourself acting and feeling differently.

# Take the opportunity today to pace yourself.

I was always a sprinter at school. I hated the cross country run. I'd get all wheezy and out of breath, it was miserable. Then, a few years back I did a charity run. I trained for it with a friend and on the first session I started running and left her behind. I looked back and she was jogging unbelievably slowly. I waited until she caught up and teased her a little but she just stayed at that pace. I decided to jog along side. After about 20 minutes we stopped, we'd only run about a mile which was fine but I noticed that I wasn't out of breath at all. Ordinarily I would have got about half a mile in and conked out exhausted.

We paced ourselves and in so doing ran further and had enough energy left over to do it all again. It's the same with everything - pace yourself and you'll get more done, it might take you longer but you'll have energy to spare and you can just keep going. Why be in such a rush to get there that you miss the journey! Remember the Hare and the Tortoise?

> *" Life is its own jour-ney, presupposes its own change and movement, and one tries to arrest them at one's eternal peril. "*
>
> - Laurens van der Post

JULY 14th

# Take the opportunity today to be a verb and not a noun.

In his brilliant 'devotional' book: *'Ideas Are Free Execution Is Priceless'*, Scott Ginsberg says it brilliantly:

*"A verb is anything that expresses <u>action</u> or <u>being</u>.* [My underline] *It could be a word. But it could also be an idea. Or a person. Or a product. Or an entire organisation."*

He goes on to say:

*"The point is: Nouns aren't noticed."*

Basically what Scott is getting at is 'verb' *people* are <u>active</u>. They are *being* what or who they want to be and they're *doing* things that they want to do.

'Noun' people on the other hand are passive - they just describe.

Ask a *'noun'* teacher who they are and they might say 'I'm a teacher.' But ask a *'verb'* teacher who they are and they might say "I teach children how they can be who they want to be and that they can achieve anything they set their minds to.'

So, are you a verb or a noun?

To find out more about Scott Ginsberg visit:
**www.HelloMyNameIsScott.com**

JULY 15th

# Take the opportunity today to ask yourself what your life would look like if it was better!

*Dream!*

Go on...indulge yourself and imagine your life as if it was perfect. Imagine every day was fulfilling to you. You smiled *all* the time. Notice what things are different in your imaginings to how they are in your present reality. Do you have more money? Do you have loving and fulfilling relationships? Do you live somewhere different?

Take as long as you like to imagine this life. As you get clearer on what it looks like and all the little details become apparent you are actually creating memories. Memories of your life to come. Your brain will actually start to *notice* circumstances that are in synch with these memories. A bit like when you buy a certain car and then see those cars everywhere. Your mind is *noticing* them. As your mind notices favourable circumstances to your new memories you may find opportunities arising where they never did before. ACT on those opportunities and they will gradually make your dream life appear IN reality.

Following on from yesterday I envisioned I was running a program based on this book. It was a program designed to help people alter their mindset. I was using the book as the basis for the program. I imagined myself in front of a room full of people - I got a real buzz just thinking about it. Pretty soon I was thinking about how I would start it, where I could run it from, how I would get people to hear about it. Tomorrow I will start writing it all down because I'm now determined to make it a reality. Watch this space!

JULY 16th
# Take the opportunity today
# to learn a new game.

'All work and no play makes Jack a dull boy', - so the saying goes. I don't know about you but I like to play games, especially with a group of close friends and family. Even more especially if there's a bottle of red wine on the table! Often we can get bored though with playing the same games. Often the same person wins, the same person comes last and so on. That's fine, the familarity itself can be part of the fun. Trying a new game from time to time can inject a new level of fun. Who knows who will be best at the new game? Who knows, it might be the most fun game you've ever played.

One thing is for sure, your favourite game at the moment was once a *new* game to you. Trying this will be another exercise in getting out of old habits, it's easy to do and fun so relax and have a go.

I didn't learn a new game but I did start writing the outline of the program to go along with this book. I love to help people in any way that I can - I guess it makes me feel valued, noticed, important, clever, revered or just appreciated. I'm sure it's a mixture of all of those feelings. But hey - win-win is the way forward right. The person I help gets something and I get something. I'll keep you posted with the progress. :D

JULY 17th

# Take the opportunity today to decide.

One way or another, decide. You can probably think of something right now as you read this that you are procrastinating over. Take a moment and consider whether you have all the information you need in order to decide. If you do, what's the hold up? Why are you not deciding?

If you're afraid that you might make the wrong decision realise that not making a decision is actually making a decision. What's the worst that can happen? Write it down. Now, what's the best that can happen? Write that down. Does the best outway the worst or vice versa?

In answering that question you should get some clarity around this point.

I've been wanting to start swimming for ages. I don't feel as fit as I want to at the moment so I need to exercise more. I also wanted to stretch every day - still haven't got around to that either. Today I'm deciding to start with the stretching. I know it's going to be good for me, I've just been lazy! Swimming, guaranteed in the next week I'm going to start. Done. Decided.

# Take the opportunity today to spend 67 minutes changng the world around you.

18th July is Nelson Mandela's birthday. As part of a global celebration of his life and influence around the world there is a movement called '67 Minutes'. The idea is that on the 18th July each year people from around the world spend 67 minutes changing the world where THEY are. Google it and find out more. It could be helping a neighbour or picking up litter or volunteering at a charity or soup kitchen etc.

I encourage you to use this opportunity to make a difference in your immediate world. The people you meet whilst you're getting involved in this *could* change your life.

JULY 19th
# Take the opportunity today
# to ask Why you want success.

What a dumb question I hear you say.

But think about it. Most people think it's about the money. To a certain degree it is, but only in the sense of what freedoms the money could bring. For instance if you wanted more money but it meant working twice as hard and having no time to see your family or friends then the money would be detrimental to your quality of life.

So, it's what you would *do* with the money that determines what your success might look like. And remember your success may be completely different than your neighbour's or your best friend's version. Give this some deep thought. Ask yourself what would you be doing if you were as successful as you wanted to be. Whose lives would you be influencing positively. At the end of the day, if you had all the money you could spend and you'd been around the world half a dozen times. Been everywhere and done everything. Taken a couple of years to just relax and persue leisure activities to your heart's content. Then what? Think about that now, don't wait *until*.

Don't wait *until* you see it happen - *see it* until it happens.

Lastly, ask yourself 'What do I lack now that success will bring me?'

---

I did the Passion Test with Em this evening at the pub (where there are no distractions). I think she got a lot out of it - clarity for one thing. I think she was surprised by the answers she came up with. I had another go myself and reinforced the desire to help people make a positive change in their lives whilst feeling a sense of freedom myself was top of the list.

---

# Take the opportunity today to decide what you would do with £10m.

So following on from yesterday's guide, if you haven't done this already - consider this today. Get a pad and start writing what you'd do with the money. I bet the list will be long - it's a lot of money!

The exercise is not so much about the cash but rather once you've done everything the cash allows you to, what do you do next? You give half a million to your parents, another half a million to your kids. You split another million and pay off the mortgages of your closest other family and friends. You buy yourself the home of your dreams and a couple of beautiful cars - maybe a boat. You give a load to your favourite charities etc.

Maybe you get to the end of the list and there's still a million left over. Do you decide to set up a business? Do you create your own charity? Whatever you decide to do there at the end - stop!

Now ask yourself what is stopping you starting that thing right now? Is it really the money that you need to start? Is it?

Only you can answer that.

JULY 21st

# Take the opportunity today to decide what success looks like for you.

Of course it's easy to imagine the nice big house, the car you've always dreamed of, holidays in exotic places and beautiful clothes. But look a little deeper and what would you be doing if you were successful? Let's imagine you've been around the world and seen everything you wanted to see. You've spent a couple of years just relaxing and indulging in all of your hobbies and pastimes and you've come home. Now what? This is similar to yesterday I know, but I really want you to look closely at this.

Really think about this today because the answer to the question could reveal a lot about who you *are*, who you want to *be* and what you want to *do*. When all the other 'desire' clutter is out of the way you are left with <u>purpose</u>.

What does *your* version of success look like?

# Take the opportunity today
# to eat something new.

How many times have you sat down to eat the same old meal that you have time and again? We know what we like and we like what we know, right? But before you knew what you liked you must of just tried stuff. Remember really enjoying the flavour of new wonderful food? Maybe you tried food from another culture. Usually when that happens you're either in another country or your in an ethnic restaurant or you may be around a friend or colleague's house. Either way part of the food experience IS the culture. It's in the surroundings and the traditions. How many people do you know that want to use chopsticks when they eat Chinese food? I know I do. It just feels more authentic.

Anyway, foreign food is one way of trying something new but often there are foods from different parts of our own culture that we haven't tried. Try some today and appreciate the culture difference aswell as the food difference.

JULY 23rd

# Take the opportunity today to ask yourself what you would do if you knew you couldn't fail.

This is a great thought exercise as long as you let your imagination be as wild as possible. No holds barred, think BIG!

By allowing your conscious mind to explore the possiblities (and what you think are impossiblities), you allow your subconscious mind to offer up ideas too. This is important as it's your subconscious mind that holds a lot of the information you might need to actually take action on any of your ideas.

If your spouse or significant other or maybe a trusted friend want to join in over a glass of wine, then it can become a lot of fun. Set some rules that keep all options open and possible, keep all comments positive - this should be fun, that's the best way to make it creative.

JULY 24th

# Take the opportunity today to express your anger next time you feel it.

Anger is a natural emotion. Like all natural emotions, if suppressed it can distort into more destructive behaviour. There are ways of dissipating anger when you feel it welling up such as meditating or just slow, deep breathing. Sometimes though it happens too suddenly - when you stub your toe for instance or maybe your computer crashes, deleting an hour's work in the process. At times like these our house can become blue with my choice of language! My other half usually keeps her office door closed due to the volume of that language in case she's on a call. I'm working on it!

The thing is, once I've screamed for a couple of seconds I calm right down - sometimes it might last for a minute or so. I rarely fester on something however. Through expessing my anger I can get through it very quickly and can therefore find clarity of mind on the other side.

I remember a scene in the Billy Crystal and Robert de Niro film 'Analyze This' - where Billy, the mafia boss' psychiatrist, tells him to *hit the pillow* on the sofa (to express his anger) and de Niro pulls out a gun and shoots the pillow into a billowing puff of stuffing! Hilarious! If you haven't seen it - treat yourself.

The big key here is - don't allow the expression of your anger to hurt or intimidate another person. It's *your* anger - *you* keep it! If you find that you tend towards anger then I suggest you seek some professional advice as it can lead to physical disease. Remember, exercise can releave the tension of anger so go for a walk to relax.

JULY 25th

# Take the opportunity today to buy something for someone for no reason.

Of course we're all used to buying birthday gifts and Christmas gifts and maybe even Valentine gifts, but how often do we get something for someone for no other reason than we saw something and thought of them. This gesture goes a long way to reminding that other person that they are on our mind.

Imagine for a moment how nice you'd feel if suddenly you were given an unexpected gift. It wouldn't have to be big or expensive, in fact it could have the same affect if it were small and silly. As long as it was relevant to you you'd be over the moon wouldn't you.

Give someone else that feeling today - it might be as simple as their favourite coffee from Starbucks.

I did this today and it really made an impact. Let me explain, I went out to the post office earlier and found my other half doing the front garden. She was getting away from work for a bit as it was 'doing her head in'. Whilst out I bought her a DVD that I knew she would enjoy. I got home and was received by some more than sarcastic comments about how it was *my* job to weed the front garden. Wanting to avoid a confrontation as I knew this had more to do with her job than with the weeds I went inside and left the DVD on her office chair. Minutes later she came back in, went to her office, then a few seconds later she came into my office and hugged me. *That* was money well spent! :)

JULY 26th

# Take the opportunity today to go to a high point and just look out.

Whether it's a hillside or a high building it doesn't matter. What matters is the view. If it's a great view then you're going to have a similar experience. I do this when I need to feel that feeling of awe. It makes me catch my breath, sometimes I get a tingling feeling down my spine. It's difficult to explain but you know what I'm talking about don't you?

There's something deeply primal about looking out to a distant horizon, maybe it's a territorial thing, maybe it's a security thing - a caveman may have felt safe being able to see all around him for any dangers for instance.

Whatever it is - I love it. I'm guessing a part of you does too.

Enjoy.

There's an area in North London called Northolt. The council there have built 3 large earth mounds for the public to enjoy. I took a walk up the tallest. The view was of the city and suburbs surrounding it but in the distance I could see other natural hills covered in woodland. I took it in for a few minutes feeling thoroughly recharged. Not the best view I've ever seen but good enough to satisfy that hunger inside of me.

# Take the opportunity today to STOP moaning!

OK - moaning can be therapeutic. Getting something off your chest can relieve the pressure and stress of a situation. We all have bad days at work. We all have encounters with rude or obnoxious people from time to time - so go ahead and moan about it. But not ALL the time. Not only are you going to relive those scenarios over and over, you're going to relive those 'feelings' over and over. And guess what, you didn't like those feelings the first time around so why do you want to experience them again and again? Moan once if you really need to then <u>stop</u>.

You'll end up wearing your friends or partners out if you become an habitual moaner so why not give them permission to stop you. Make some rules maybe - like if they've heard that story before you can't tell them again, or if it's about the same person, they can ask you to stop. You get the idea. Be aware though that if they follow through and ask you to stop - you can't then moan at *or* about them for doing it.

JULY 28th

# Take the opportunity today to make a list of things you're not good at - now work on them.

Most of us can be self critical at the drop of a hat so I'm guessing it won't take long to write this list. The time, and therefore effort, is spent working on them. Make it easier on yourself by just trying to work on one at a time. Give yourself a chance. You may just find that with a little perseverance you are better at somethings than you thought. Then you may find opportunities presenting themselves where you never thought to notice before.

**" If you want to truly understand something, try to change it. "**

\- Kurt Lewin

# Take the opportunity today to accept things the way they are. It doesn't stop you changing them.

There's a psychological process that we all suffer from on occasion: Attachment.

Attachment is the holding on to an outcome of some kind. Let's say you're trying to get a new job and you see the perfect position for you advertised in the paper. You apply and you get an interview. The interview goes well and they say they'll let you know within a week if you have the job. Meantime your boss in your present job rubs you up the wrong way and you begin to 'hope' that you get the new position. This hope is fine up until the point when you get a phone call or letter saying unfortunately you didn't get the job. At that point your mood sinks, you become depressed at the thought of going in to work the next day. You become miserable at the thought of being stuck in a job you hate.

You have become 'attached' to the outcome of getting a new job. You have made your happiness dependant on getting that position and when that doesn't happen you spiral into a bad mood.

The healthier thing to do is 'accept' the situation. Just accept that you didn't get that job and continue looking for another position. Accept that until you find another job you'll have to keep working at your present one. You're still looking to change that situation. But through accepting it you can remain calm and focused.

A lot of upset in our lives is caused by our attachment to outcomes whether it's being stuck in traffic which is making us late for something, or builders not turning up when they agreed which means your kitchen won't be fitted today, or whether the person you wanted to ask for a date is now going out with someone else.

They are all attachments to the outcome. Some are harder to accept than others but practice will help. Start today accepting things the way they are and the way they turn out, then, continue trying to change them. Calmly and with determined focus.

Remember: we can't control everything that happens *to us*, but we can control how we react *to it*.

# Take the opportunity today to take The Passion Test.

Chris & Janet Attwood created The Passion Test as an easy to use tool to understand more fully what we truly desire. I thoroughly recommend you investigate further - buy the book even, because I cannot do the process justice here in just two pages.

Having said that, what I will do is explain my experience of doing The Passion Test, which is a powerful exercise in getting 'clear'. Clear about what it is you want in your life. As the Attwoods say *"Passion is about how you live your life. Goals are what you choose to create in your life."*

So I started by making a list of five things I am passionate about. As instructed I started each with the words: *"When I am living my ideal life I am..."* Then, I got Em to ask me the following: If you could have your #1 Passion but *not* your #2 Passion which would you choose? Then, if you could have your #1 Passion but *not* your #3 Passion which would you choose? And so on. The idea is that you really do have to think of having one *or* the other, but not both. In choosing, you get a bit clearer. In doing this you'll probably find it a bit difficult to choose sometimes - but choose you <u>must</u>!

You should end up with your five Passions in order of how important they are to you. So then I tried it with 10 Passions. If you do this process a few times you should end up with a really good idea of what you are most passionate about in your life. After that do the test every few months to see if things have changed.

Once I discovered my #1 Passion I went to step two and made a list of actions I could take to move towards it. Once this list was done I went through the comparing process as per the passions list. That is, asking if I could take action #1 but *not* #2 which would I choose. This made it clearer which actions I should take and in which order.

If you decide to do this, whenever you are faced with either a decision, choice or opportunity, always choose in favour of your Passions. Ask yourself each time: 'Will this move me towards my Passions or away?'

Scott Ginsberg has another insightful way of judging whether one of your interests is actually a Passion - he suggests you ask yourself two questions about it:

1. What are you prepared to suffer to do this?
2. Would it cause you suffering if you did not do it?

To find out more about The Passion Test and the work of Chris and Janet Attwood go to: **www.ThePassionTest.com**.

My number 1 Passion seems to be making a positive difference in other people's lives whilst feeling free myself. Chris & Janet would say this is cheating because I'm putting two things as my first passion 'feeling free' and 'helping others' - so I guess I need to spend some time and do it again, and again until it feels spot on. That's why I urge you to check the book out for yourself. It's fun and very revealing, trust me!

JULY 31st

# Take the opportunity today to review the guides of this month to see which ones you may have missed.

We're over halfway through the year now and I sincerely hope you have noticed some changes in your life since reading this book and implementing it's guides. Keep going over the month's guides as often as you can to give yourself the best chance of noticing one that will grab your attention. It's those guides that grab you that you should put most effort into doing. There are literally hundreds in this book so I'm 100% certain many will prove useful, inspirational, motivational and ultimately life changing.

---

Make a note in your journal or diary of any changes you have noticed since you started this book.

---

AUGUST 1st

# Take the opportunity today to change your frequency.

Mary Morrissey is a renowned life coach and spiritual teacher who has shared the stage with the Dalai Lama and many other incredibly inspiring individuals. One of her core techniques is to get you to 'change frequency'. The way she describes it is beautiful. We are surrounded by an infinite quantity of frequencies in the same way we are surrounded by TV and Radio waves. In order to watch something different on the TV or listen to something different on the radio we simply 'change channel' (change frequency).

We can do this with our feelings too. We can change the channel from feeling miserable to euphoric, or from afraid to confident just by changing the frequency we're tuned into. She describes it as going from CNN (Constantly Negative News) to the Discovery Channel.

What a great way to look at it.

What would you like to see and feel on *your* Discovery Channel?

So, how to actually do that... One way I learnt from Tony Robbins is to change your Triad. Revisit p.74 to remind yourself of that brilliant strategy. Try that for a start.

To find out more about Mary Morrissey visit:
**www.MaryMorrissey.com**

AUGUST 2nd

# Take the opportunity today to be truthful in every way.

I'm going to guess that this is going to be a difficult one for most people. Let's be *honest*, we're all untruthful in some way or another every day. Maybe to get ourselves out of a sticky situation, maybe *to* ourselves *about* a sticky situation. Often we do the little white lie because we think it will spare someone's feelings. In a way we're programmed that some lying is ok from an early age - did your parents tell you Santa was real for instance? Then, as we were growing up we heard the lies our parents would tell and maybe for the best of reasons: *'Don't tell mummy we got her a birthday present - it's a secret.'* They seem harmless and to a certain extent they are, possibly though they embed in us from a young age that some lying is good. Try to resist this programming today, try to be truthful to everyone in every way.

Being truthful also has wider connotations - for instance, going to find a shop assistant when we've broken something by accident instead of just walking away. Or, having integrity and fairness and a sense of responsibility, these are all ways of being truthful.

Good luck - you'll need it! (We all will.)

PS: If you do have to tell a truth today where you'd normally tell a white lie, tread softly.

# Take the opportunity today to learn.

Learning is a passion of mine. When I was at school however, I found many of the lessons dull, boring, mundane and tedious. Subjects that today I find fascinating; history, geography, biology, science, literature. It boils down to the way we learn. At school these subjects were taught out of text books or via the blackboard. Groan! I wasn't engaged, my imagination wasn't stirred.

Maybe it's an age thing, that as we get older we become more interested in the world at large and how it got that way. But I don't think so. Bob Proctor said once that a child, up to the age of five or six, would rather learn than do *anything*. If you think about it a child's brain is programmed to learn just as a matter of survival.

Considering our brain grows more outside of the womb than the nine months inside it, which is more than any other animal, suggests that learning is the most valuable asset we have. Intelligence however is the result of the cumulation of knowledge whereas wisdom is the result of experience. If we allow experience and knowledge to combine we can take our learning to new heights. This learning will allow us to take advantage of more opportunitites which in turn will give us new experiences. If we continue to learn from *them* - hopefully we'll get a little wiser in the process.

# Take the opportunity today to teach.

Following on from yesterday's guide of 'learning', today I suggest you consider teaching. The reason is that through teaching we can actually increase our own learning. We get to see the subject in finer detail. Take the martial arts for example, when you attain black belt status you are considered a teacher. What this actually means is you are ready to really learn. The great martial arts masters knew that through teaching their techniques they were able to hone them over and over. Their techniques improved through the process of teaching. As each new student asked 'how' a certain technique was implemented the master had to drill down into greater and greater detail in order to help the student understand. By doing this the master *noticed* in greater detail what he actually did to implement the technique.

You don't need to be a complete expert either before you start teaching. If you have something to share, start there. As you teach it to others your own understanding will deepen and before too long you will become an expert. Become the black belt in your chosen field by teaching others what you know. Be generous and show them everything and remember, their questions will help to teach *you* in the process.

I read somewhere that if we hear something we retain approx 5% of the information, if we see and hear we retain up to 20%, if we see, hear and do we retain up to 50%, but if we teach we retain up to 90% of the information. Teaching really is the way to learn!

AUGUST 5th

# Take the opportunity today to look how far you have come.

Every now and then I get into the 'I haven't achieved enough/done enough/seen enough/created enough' mode. You know the one?

Give yourself a break. Think back 10 years, where were you?

My guess is - not as far along as you are now. Maybe you're in a bigger home or driving a nicer car or you're earning more income. I would imagine you've seen a bit more of the world than 10 years ago and certainly had more experiences - good or bad.

Give it some thought and you'll realise you've come quite a way, maybe it's not as far as you thought or hoped for, but it's at least further along the road. Allow how far you've come to inspire you to go further rather than holding you back.

If you are reading this and you are actually further back from where you were 10 years ago then remember where you've been, how you got there and resolve to get there again. You've done it once already - second time around is usually easier because you've learnt from all the mistakes and wrong turns you took the first time.

AUGUST 6th

# Take the opportunity today to allow yourself to change your mind about something.

Pretty easy request wouldn't you say? Brighton are a rubbish football team, or maybe not. Olives are disgusting! But have you ever tried eating them IN a dish rather than on their own? I need to go abroad for my holidays this year. Really? Have you even looked at the beautiful opportunities to get away there are in your own country - maybe even on your own doorstep?

We can change our mind any*time* about any*thing*. We just need to look at why we think a particular way sometimes.

Give this some thought and change your mind about something today.

## " *Change always comes bearing gifts.* "

- Price Pritchett

AUGUST 7th

# Take the opportunity today to allow yourself to change your belief about something.

Following on from yesterday changing your beliefs can be a bit trickier. Our beliefs are in charge of our decisions. If you want to change your decision making process you need to take a good look at your beliefs. Take some time to consider what influences you are allowing to affect your beliefs. What papers are you reading? What news stations are you watching or listening to? What do your friends and family believe about certain things? All these have influence over what *you* believe.

What beliefs do you have that are either the same as or in contradiction to your parents or even grandparents? Many people will reject the beliefs of these authority figures as a form of rebellion. Those beliefs may become ingrained although years later you may actually believe differently. So how do you know? You need to ask delving questions like: 'Why do I believe [xyz]?' and 'Am I sure that my belief in [xyz] is sound?' or 'What evidence do I have for believing [xyz]?'

It's possible to change a belief in an instant, as with many other changes, it's the getting ready that takes the time.

AUGUST 8th

# Take the opportunity today to be open.

This is difficult for a lot of people - yes, me included. When you're 'open' you are vulnerable. We don't like to feel vulnerable, it's in our genes to keep ourselves safe. When we lived in caves it meant being physically safe from a bear or a wolf or even our tribe. I would imagine that a wrong look in those days could have been looked upon as confrontational. (Still does in some places.) So, we began to hide what we were thinking lest it showed on our face.

In today's sophisticated society a facial expression is still a measure of what we might be thinking consciously *or* subconsciously. So we find more and more ways to try and keep our thoughts and feelings covered up, private.

Today, find a safe environment to be open. With a family member or a best friend or anyone you trust. Start there. I think you'll find that with some practice you'll prefer to be open often. We're not talking over-sharing here by the way! It's a bit indulgent to offer gratuitous information so understand *why* you're being open. This is about suppressed feelings that might be causing blocks in your life - not sharing the gory details of your gall bladder operation. :)

Remember, if you need to be open with someone about *their* behaviour, tread carefully and speak kindly.

AUGUST 9th
# Take the opportunity today to STOP lying.

There's a subtle difference between being truthful (Aug 2nd) and not lying. Lying is about deliberate deceit. We all do it. OK, maybe the Dalai Lama doesn't, maybe Mother Theresa didn't, but the rest of us DO!

We lie to our spouses:
"Honey, does my bum look big in this?"
"No! You look great." [Lie]

We lie to our friends:
"So I told her to shove her job, you'd have done the same, right?"
"Sure I would." [Lie]

We lie to our colleagues:
"How you feeling today - getting any better?"
"No (*croak*), need another day off I think." [Lie]

We lie to ourselves:
"I could never do that, could I?"
"No way, you're better off staying where you are - it's safer!" [Lie]

Spend today being ultra aware of what you say and determine if everything is the truth, the whole truth and nothing but the truth. And yes, white lies are lies so if your offspring ask where babies come from think about your answer carefully. :)

Once again - good luck, you'll need it!

AUGUST 10th

# Take the opportunity today to enjoy the journey.

Did you watch Kelly Holmes winning her two Gold Medals in the 2004 Olympics? If not, go and watch them now - it's inspirational, here's a link to the YouTube video: **http://tinyurl.com/42uaukd** Now, imagine if someone had said to her before each race 'Hey Kelly, you can have the Gold Medal, we know you're the best, there's no need to run.' do you think she would have replied: 'Oh, great, thanks - I'll get changed into my tracksuit then.'? - <u>I don't think so!</u>

The journey is the *experience* you are having, the race is the challenge and the medal is the prize - the medal without the race means nothing and the race without the journey means nothing. And I don't think it's about competing. I don't think it's about beating other people. I think it's about proving something to yourself.

So my question to you is: What prize are you after, and at what stage of the race are you in? If you haven't started yet that's ok - preparation is an important part of the process! If you don't do the prep you won't get past the first hurdle. Having said that, there's only so much prep you can do. You can't win the prize until you enter the race. Some of you I guess are already well in to the second or third laps, maybe you can even see the finishing line. Well done you! If you're struggling though and feel that you're not going to make it, dig deep, think of that podium, think of the roaring crowd, see yourself winning. This is your journey, this is your race and you can get that medal - but you have to keep going.

<u>And remember</u>: it's the journey that's important because the only *real* finish line is the last one, if you know what I mean!

# Take the opportunity today to fully appreciate something or someone.

When was the last time you really stopped and appreciated your car or your washing machine or your kettle or your computer or your TV? Think about it, how often do we find ourselves shouting and maybe swearing at things when they don't work how they should. My poor computer definitely comes in for a verbal bashing sometimes!

But how often do you appreciate it when it works perfectly - which is probably most of the time?

Our washing machine went kaput the other day which was a pain because then we had to do the whole searching for a replacement. It took days of hunting websites and magazines and shops before we finally chose one - meanwhile the washing was piling up. It was when we started talking with the sales reps in one store that we realised how well our old machine had done in lasting 12 years. We just take stuff for granted don't we?

Now consider if there is someONE that you don't appreciate anywhere near as much as you should. And if you do, do you tell them? If the answer to that is no, or not enough, then change that today.

Let them know they are appreciated

# Take the opportunity today to examine how you feel.

What kind of mood are you in? Funny sort of question isn't it? What mood are you in?

If you're IN a mood - good, bad or indifferent - then it stands to reason that you can get OUT of that mood. But did you realise that You can *choose* to get in or out of a mood?

Imagine for a moment that you receive a phone call. It's the tax man and he tells you that your tax has been incorrectly calculated and you owe them £10,000. Holy cow! And he wants it by the end of the week or you'll get a further £1000 fine. How would you feel? Pretty upset and anxious I would bet. Then the phone rings again. It's the tax man, he apologises and says he read it incorrectly and actually they owe You £10,000. Woohoo! Now how do you feel? You start dancing around the room, then the phone goes again. Yep, you guessed it - the tax man again. He apologises profusely, he got the wrong name and it's actually someone else who is owed the £10,000. Now how do you *feel*? Bit of a roller-coaster right?

The thing is, at no time were you under physical threat and at no time were you having an exciting experience. It was all happening in your mind. You were having the thoughts about how you were going to *raise* £10k then, how you were going to *spend* £10k.

So examine how you're feeling today and ask yourself *why* you're feeling that way. What thoughts are creating *that* feeling. Just be aware is all. That simple exercise can often help you find calmness when you need it.

AUGUST 13th

# Take the opportunity today to be assertive.

How many times have you become frustrated with a situation or person simply because *you* weren't assertive enough about your involvement? I can certainly remember many times. Sometimes it's because I didn't say no to something I should have and sometimes it's because I said yes to something I shouldn't have. Ever had that? Well, today, before you answer yes or no to something think if it's really what you want to do, or at least if it's something you could live with without any resentment. If it isn't, then find the kindest way you can to say 'No I can't do that.' or 'Do you know what, this is what I actually want.' It's perfectly acceptable to be assertive as long as it's not aggressive or intimidating. It's just standing your ground. Putting your foot down.

This morning my other half wanted a lie in (it's Sunday). I had planned to wake at 8am and doze for a while. About 7:30am one of the dogs started wimpering so I got up to let her out and fed the cat whilst I was there. Then went back to bed only to find 5 minutes later the other dog moaning at me - so I got up and let him out. Then came back to bed. He followed back up to bed and started moaning for Em to rise. Em looked at me sleepily and said "I thought you were getting up early?" Meaning: get up and take these pets with you so I can sleep. "No" I said, "I just wanted to wake up - not get up!" She got up with a huff because 'her' lie in was ruined. OK, I could have just done it but this morning I had 'planned' to lie in and daydream a little. I ended up agreeing that if she tells me next time *before we go to bed*, that she needs a lie in the following morning, to tell me and I'll ensure she gets it. No harm done.

AUGUST 14th

# Take the opportunity today to plan a trip.

You may be lucky enough to be working in a job you love, but you still need to get away from it all from time to time. For those of you who don't particularly like their job or maybe don't even have a job, getting away from it all is even more necessary. The usual excuse for those who are busy is they don't have time and for those without a job it's I can't afford it. Well here's a question for you:

1) For those of you that are too busy, what would happen if you were hit by the proverbial bus tomorrow? What would happen at work? Would it get done by someone else? Whatever catastophe happened would it turn out all right in the end? Of course it would. Maybe you own your own business and you're the only one there. Would your clients all desert you if you took a week off? (If the answer to that is yes by the way - you need to look for better clients!)

The point is, life will go on and everything will be just fine if you took a week off to have some time for yourself.

2) For those who can't afford it - you don't have the excuse of worrying about work but you don't have to 'pay' to get away. Surely you can visit some friends or family even for a few days. Borrow a tent and go camp in a field. Take the bus to somewhere you don't normally go and explore. We're talking pennies here.

The important thing is to get away from our present surroundings. When we do this we get a chance to see things in a different light, from a different angle. We can have thoughts that we don't usually have. 'A change is as good as a rest' someone once said, and that's exactly what a holiday (of any sort *or* duration) is all about.

# Take the opportunity today to learn the GOLF lesson.

If you've ever felt like you don't have enough time to get everything done that you need to do on a daily basis then try this strategy devised by the Internet Marketing/Property genius - Dean Jackson.

In a nutshell Dean identifies 4 Reactive Activator areas common to most of us:

**1. Email   2. The phone   3. People   4. Thoughts**

These are the most common distractors we face daily.

Dean devised the **GOLF** strategy to combat them.

| | |
|---|---|
| **G**oal | - set yourself a task you want to complete |
| **O**ptimal Environment | - go to where you're most likely to get that done |
| **L**imited Distractions | - remove anything that will distract you, phones, computers, etc. |
| **F**ixed Timescale | - set a timer for how long you need |

The analogy is that if you decided to play a round of golf you'd have to set aside approx. 4 hours of your time to do that. Whilst you're playing golf for 4 hours you're not able to email, or phone, or get bugged by colleagues (as long as you turn your mobile device off).

The tricky part is eliminating your thought distractions. For this he suggests spending 50 minutes writing down as many thoughts as you can, big, small, weird, irrelevant, important - whatever! This now reduces the chance you will have a rogue thought distract you while you're doing your task.

I can't do this justice here without writing a few pages so I suggest you check out his video (if it's still available) at:

**http://bit.ly/nBVvaw**

In it he explains and clarifies the whole process.

AUGUST 16th
# Take the opportunity today to be aware of your breathing.

Every now and then stop and notice your breathing. You don't have to slip into meditation mode (although if you have the time I recommend it), just notice. Are you breathing shallow and quickly? Are you holding your breath without realising? Are you huffing and puffing?

If it's any of those then take a second to relax. Shrug your shoulders two or three times. Take a deep breath and let it out slowly.

Notice a few times today and you may find that your breathing is keeping you tense. Regulate it and you'll calm down almost immediately.

AUGUST 17th

# Take the opportunity today to be aware of your thoughts.

We each have countless thousands of thoughts every day, but how many are we actually aware of? Of course we're aware of them as we think them but are we aware that we're aware? Sounds like a dumb question but bare with me a second. When you have a thought about something or maybe someone, obviously you're conscious of the act of thinking at that moment. However, the true awareness comes when you start to think about *why* you're having that thought. For example maybe you got angry seeing someone throw litter from a car, you had the thought of how ignorant they must be spoiling the environment like that. Now examine *why* you thought that. Could it be because you hate to see litter on the floor but it's not your job to pick it up, so it's going to stay there and make the place look dirty and untidy? You may feel guilty that you too are going to leave it there. Or maybe you are affected by the laziness of the litterbug, you're not lazy so why are they?

Whatever your thought is, think about *why* you're having it. It might say more about you than you realise. Try and get past the justifying thoughts and get deep down into the core reasons why you think that way.

AUGUST 18th

# Take the opportunity today to finish something you have started.

It could be a book that's been hanging around for a while. It could be the de-cluttering of that room you started a couple of weeks ago, or a hundred other things.

The important thing is to go finish it - today! Then decide that that was the impetus for finishing a lot of stuff that's half done in your life. Start finishing things, get in to the habit of seeing stuff through to completion. All the loose ends in our lives can really be stressful. We have *real* 'to do' lists and we have *virtual* 'to do' lists.

You know how good you feel when most of the stuff is ticked off on your physical list, think how good you'll feel when your *mind* is clearer of things to do too.

There'll be more space to think.

AUGUST 19th

# Take the opportunity today to think about something you'd like to change about yourself.

This was the life changing moment for me. (See my Case Study p.76) A few years ago I met a hypnotherapist at an alternative health centre open day. He's also an NLP practitioner. I got the opportunity to sit with him for 40 minutes or so to experience a sample of what he does. He started by asking the question above: *'If you could change one thing about yourself today, what would it be?'*

Not expecting the question, I said the first thing that came into my head (I have since realised that is how to get the subconscious mind to speak) which was: *'I'd like to make better decisions quicker.'*

He then took me through a series of mental exercises, visualisations and 'make believes'. The result was a feeling of euphoric realisation as I walked the short distance home. I *was* going to make decisions quicker, in fact I had just *decided* that - right there and then!

The man's name is Mick McEvoy and you can learn more about him and what he does by going to: **www.YourCalmCoach.co.uk**

Thanks again Mick! :)

---

Today I am going to think about how I can change any limiting beliefs I have about my ability to succeed as a writer. I saw this amazing video of Tony Robbins discussing why people don't implement - with Frank Kern and John Reese, two giants in the Internet Marketing arena. Tony reveals that the main reason is people want certainty. But they can only really get that from 'seeing' the results they want _before_ they take any action. Great video! If you want to see it visit my Be Inspired blog: **www.conversations-with-blog.blogspot.com** and search for 'Great Tony Robbins interview' in the Aug '11 file.

---

AUGUST 20th

# Take the opportunity today to be resourceful.

This is the most valuable quality someone can have if you ask me. The term 'resourceful' can apply to what you might need to survive. It can apply to what you might need to succeed in business. It might apply to what you might need in order to have the relationships that you desire.

If you are a resourceful person you can get anything done. Start every problem solving moment with the question: 'How can I..." and allow your mind to go off and find the answer. Before you know it you'll be thinking of all sorts of ways to get to where you want to be.

As you find your own ways of being resourceful write them down. Keep them handy and apply them to every situation you find your-self stuck in. You can use the same mindset that you use in business as you do in your relationships - you'll have to put a new angle on it but the strategy will work.

Keep in mind the Neale Donald Walsch saying: *'The quickest way to get what you want is to help someone else get it first.'*

I had the idea for a mindset changing program (back in July) to help people (my readers mainly) alter the way they think in order to maximise their potential. It's starting to take shape - I think it will compliment this book. :)

# Take the opportunity today to help someone else be resourceful.

So, following on from yesterday, if you discovered ways to become more resourceful - share them. Find someone else that might be struggling with some issue or another and offer your insights to them. They may reject them, and that's ok. It might not be a one size fits all or they might not be ready for those insights yet.

Accept the way people react to your trying to help. It's easy to feel upset, or angry or disappointed that someone doesn't follow your good advice. But let it go. You tried.

Most people *will* accept help when offered so keep offering. And if you can help them become more resourcful you will have given them something invaluable.

AUGUST 22nd

# Take the opportunity today to confront another one of your fears.

Way back on March 24th I suggested you do this. I don't know if you did or not - I did, and it was an enlightening experience. Try again today whether you did in March or not. The more of your fears you confront, analyse, dissect, uncover, shine a light on and expose, the more confident you will become. You will realise at some point that *You* are the source of all your fears. Yeah, I know, some of you may have had terrible things happen in your childhood but you're not in your childhood now. You are now fully grown - physically. Time to become fully grown emotionally.

I'm not suggesting that it's easy. But it is incredibly fruitful. You'd like to live without fear wouldn't you? Go back and read March 24th if you need to but don't hesitate for too long, grab one of your fears by the scruff of the neck and take a good close look!

Once again I find myself sitting here wondering about my own fears. The same one springs to mind - fear of failure. We were with some friends yesterday and I was explaining the idea behind this book. Their feedback although positive made me doubt if it was a good idea after all. I started to think about it failing miserably. I dwelt on it for a minute or two then decided that I wasn't going to become attached to the outcome but that I was going to pursue this endeavour as far as I possibly could. Nobody will put me off!

AUGUST 23rd
# Take the opportunity today
# to network.

You might be good at this already - I'm not. Not naturally anyway. I always feel like I'm forcing small talk or I feel like I'm selling myself - YUK!

However, I've started to look at it in a different light recently. If I walk into a room at a networking evening or a party or a conference or a business meeting I focus on trying to help someone. That might be directly or indirectly. If indirectly, then it usually means I know someone that could help them. I then put those people in touch and hey presto - I've just networked.

So, if like me, you don't naturally enjoy networking try thinking of it as an opportunity for you to just help and serve someone. We all like helping someone out don't we?

AUGUST 24th

# Take the opportunity today to understand the law of opposing forces.

Newton's Law that states every action has an opposite and equal reaction, ie: the positive energy of gratitude you send out will come back to you. Help and be helped in return. That's not to say 'help' and expect to be 'helped' in return by that person or any other person. Just *know* that you will be helped somehow. Thank and be thanked. Give and be given.

Some of you might be thinking Newton didn't mean it that way. You might think that Newton was just talking about physical forces like the butt of a rifle forcing it's way into your shoulder with the same force that the bullet propels from the barrel. But I will argue that it's *all* energy. And if Newton was around today and got to grips with Quantum Mechanics he would agree with me. Everything is energy and therefore any form of energy is subject to his Law.

For practical uses Scott Ginsberg writes about duality in a similar way in his book 'Ideas Are Free Execution Is Priceless' (p.131) where he suggests embracing opposites in order to be successful. One example he uses is being patient with an equal amount of impatience. Patient with the process, understanding that things don't always go the way or the speed you planned and impatient enough to get moving with ideas without waiting until every tiny detail has been considered.

Think of how you could use this concept today.

# Take the opportunity today to create a vision board.

John Assaraf (star of The Secret) is the creator of the Vision Board idea. In a nutshell you get yourself a corkboard or something similar and you cover it in pictures/words and anything else to hand that represent the things you love in your life AND the things you'd love to *have* in your life.

You get magazines, newspapers, mailers, books etc. and you take the images out that best illustrate what it is you value. You pin them on the board and then keep the board in a place that you can see every day. In your office or study or kitchen or hallway, whatever, someplace that you know you'll see it every day.

Why?

The idea is that by seeing these images each and every day you allow yourself to get into the same vibration as what you see. Your dream home or car for example. Or your dream lifestyle, job or even your partner. You might want to believe that by seeing these images every day your subconscious mind ends up creating ways to help you get them.

Whatever you believe - it works! Don't get bogged down in the *how*, just try it and see.

For more info on John Assaraf go here: **www.PraxisNow.com**

Myself and Em have had our Vision Boards up in our respective offices for two or three years now, and although I need to make mine a lot bigger, I'm definitely moving towards those things I included. Yep, just took another look - it's definitely got to get bigger! :)

AUGUST 26th

# Take the opportunity today to slow down.

If you live in the western world you know exactly what I'm talking about here. Everything is a hundred miles an hour. You turn on the TV and they can't even run the credits on programmes anymore without squeezing the screen up so they can advertise the next program. The commercials have so much motion in them your eyes don't get a second to settle on anything until the pack shot at the end.

Then there's our jobs, the deadlines, the rush to get home. Sometimes I actually like to get stuck in traffic just for the chance to slow down. It doesn't help that we are now contactable 24/7 via our multi functional mobile devices. Many statistics now show that we are actually less productive than 20 years ago for this very reason.

We don't give ourselves the time to focus.

So, slow down. Just for today. And if you like it, do it again another day, and another and so on. Before too long you will be living a calmer more enjoyable and rewarding life. Believe me - you won't be missing anything.

# Take the opportunity today to change your perception.

I recently completed the Bob Proctor 'Goal Achiever's Program' and on one of the audios I listened to he spoke about perception. It supposes that our perception of a situation directly influences our action in that circumstance.

EG: We'd gladly walk across a plank of wood suspended 6 feet off the ground if there was a £1000 reward at the other end, but we wouldn't if the plank were 200 feet off the ground. Then again, if our child was in a building that was on fire and that plank bridged the gap between it and a neighbouring building we would gladly cross it to save them - no matter how high up.

I've listened to it a few times now and something dawned on me last night as I was walking one of our dogs; if that's true, which it seems obvious that it is, then we can actually use that knowledge to motivate ourselves more effectively.

Let's say you have a task to do on your day off. It's a bit of a dull task but it needs doing. You might ordinarily decide to leave it and do it another day and we all know what will happen there - the next day becomes another day which becomes another day and so on and the task remains to be done. Now consider that you put it in your mind that your boss is going to give you a 20% rise if you get that task completed today. Just *think* that. You'll possibly find that actually motivated you to consider doing the task. Really imagine it's true, imagine you just got off the phone with your boss, they were really pumped up and excited about giving you that raise for completing that task. Pretty soon you will feel a whole lot more motivated to do it.

Note: Keep the perception positive rather than negative, ie: imagine the boss is going to give you a raise for doing it rather than imagining he'll fire you for *not* doing it. Positive outcomes are much more compelling and motivational than negative ones.

Try it and see - it's just a theory!

> **" The only difference between a rut and a grave is their dimensions. "**
>
> - Ellen Glasgow

AUGUST 28th

# Take the opportunity today to go to a live event.

I for one do not go to enough live events. Maybe you do - if so excellent. If not, make the effort. They don't all cost money either. Many bars and cafes have live music as do pizza restaurants and other free to enter venues. OK, so you'll have to buy a drink and maybe eat something. Alternatively there are always festivals of all types, shapes and sizes happening along with free open air concerts.

Get Googling.

So why do I encourage this?

Because it's an expereince. We are all here, living our lives, wanting and searching for experiences. That is what life's all about isn't it? Engaging in experiences en mass heightens our enjoyment as well. I think it's because we feel more connected, another one of life's goals. Through involving yourself in these live events you will strengthen your existing relationships with those you share the experience with, give yourself the opportunity to meet new like minded people and get to reconnect with your own soul.

Myself and Em recently saw Phantom Of The Opera in the West End with some friends over from Oz. We had a lovely dinner before and drinks after and the show itself was amazing. Great experience. Want more.

# Take the opportunity today to STOP any critical self-talk.

Do you ever stub your toe and immediately shout something like: 'You stupid clumsy idiot, ahhhh!'?

Or maybe when chatting with a friend say something like: 'Oh god, I've got a terrible memory!'?

Or ever thought to yourself something like: 'Well I won't be able to do that, I'm useless when it comes to stuff like that'?

Or something similar anyway. I for one am guilty of all three. But I'm working on it. I realise that they are just my false paradigms showing through. Or my fears being announced. Every time I find myself saying negative things about myself, first I try to stop it, then if it gets out I smile, say: 'Cancel, cancel' then reverse what I said into something positive. This way, slowly but surely I'm creating new beliefs about myself. Eventually I hope to eradicate all negative self-talk from my vocabulary.

If it sounds silly, ask yourself- what harm can it do?

# Take the opportunity today to empathise.

You ever have one of those days where nothing seems to go right? Where you feel life is out to get you? Where you don't know which way to turn, you're confused or frustrated or just plain angry?

Did one of your friends or family really listen to you and say something like: 'Oh God! That's terrible.' or 'Holy cow! how did you get through that?' or 'Oh you poor thing, I don't know what I would have done in that situation.'?

They didn't try to solve anything or give you advice or tell you what you should have said or done. They just offered support and understanding. How much better did you feel after that? If it's never happened to you - imagine how you would feel if it did.

I'm hoping you said it made you feel better or would make you feel better. If that's the case then offer that to someone today if the opportunity arises. Just listen and feel how they are feeling. Imagine *You* are going through that. Let them know you understand how they feel or at least can appreciate how they feel.

Offer no solutions (unless asked for), offer no advice (unless asked for).

AUGUST 30th

# Take the opportunity today to write a letter to one of your parents.

Now I don't know what your relationship is like with your parents. But to be honest it doesn't matter whether it's good or bad, close or non-existant. Even if you've never met your parents or parent. Even if your parents or parent are no longer with us. Put pen to paper and what you want to say will come pouring out. It might take a while. You might have to just write - something, anything, but when it starts it will pour out.

This will be a cathartic exercise. It might be painful, it might be joyful but it *will be* rewarding.

You may decide to post the letter afterwards or you may not. If you don't want to I would suggest you put the letter in an envelope marked 'To Mum' or 'To Dad' or 'To Mum & Dad' and *post* it. It will never get to them but you will have symbolically sent it.

AUGUST 31st

# Take the opportunity today to review the guides of this month to see which ones you may have missed.

Another month over, did you manage to do many of the guides? I hope you did as there were some really useful ones in there. I definitely missed some good ones so I'm going back over them right now to see which ones jump out at me.

Remember, if you don't actually do any of them they can't help. You'll end up changing nothing! What would be the point? So try some, apply them and be aware of how you feel afterwards.

---

Make a note in your journal or diary of any changes you have noticed since you started this book.

---

CASE STUDY 4

# Donna's Story

It was seven months after my Mum had died, I had just had a miscarriage, my boyfriend at the time dumped me when he realised I was pregnant and my job was going no-where fast. My dearest friend Debi had moved an hour and a half's drive away and I missed her proximity and the ability to pop in and see her children, who would ground me and give me belief that life goes on and that it is more meaningful than my problems. I was probably at my lowest ebb. I went to Debi's one Friday in January for the weekend and took her a couple of bottles of wine. Work had been particularly horrible that week and when I got to Debi's I joined her in a glass of wine, which stretched to three (something I had never done because I don't drink). We had dinner and mid way through a sentence I apparently just went to sleep and not long after that, woke and promptly became violently sick. Debi's husband Martin, had to carry me to bed!

The next morning to much amusement, they all asked how I was and then 13 years of mickey taking started! They were all proud of me and the boys were upset they were not up to witness their Aunt Donna - drunk!

Well after this wee incident I decided that I clearly needed to sort myself out, not because I had had a drink for the first time in my 35 years, but because I felt my life had lost its meaning, that I wasn't in control of it. I felt rudderless and without my Mum nothing seemed really very important. The drinking just gave me the kick I needed to face facts and have a long serious chat with myself. To reflect on all that I had in my life, my family, my friends and most important to me, my god children (Josh, Ollie, Scarlett) and my niece Hannah. The joy they brought me was enormous but I also missed them when I didn't see them and this made me look at the void in my life and whether or not my relationship with these children was preventing me from finding the right person and having my own family, or simply just filling the time until I found the right person. Or, was the grief of my mother's death just so overwhelming I couldn't make head nor tail of anything. Essentially, I couldn't work out how I felt or why and questioned everything. I made a decision that I needed to be a bit kinder to myself and to allow myself to grieve for my mum in a way that I hadn't allowed myself so far and made a conscious decision to let life just be for a few months before deciding what it was that I wanted.

After a few months of reflection and not berating myself for the constant ache I felt for the loss of my mother, I actually felt stronger and made the decision to move house to be near Debi and the children and start a new life, build new interests and have a new job that excited me and where I felt I might excel. Within six weeks of this decision, I had a new job, and eight months after that I had moved house closer to my friend. My brother moved in with me for the last six months I was in my old house and my niece Hannah was with us for most weekends, which was absolutely bliss, watching her grow and getting closer to her was so rewarding. It's a period in my life that when I look back was one of my most pleasurable. The new job wasn't so great, and the house had its problems, with children breaking in, getting beaten up by them, a con woman and a burglary. But all of that was manageable and didn't actually affect me in a way that most people assumed it would. I now had the strength and courage to know it was in my power to change things and I had the power to control how I felt. It was up to me to be a victim or not, and I have chosen never to be a victim.

I am now truly happy and contented! The knowledge and belief that it was me who controlled my destiny and not others and that I had the power to change, has meant that I now roll with the waves. Being open to new opportunities and not allowing myself to be trapped by circumstance, has meant that when I finally met the person I couldn't live without, I didn't overlook him because I was pre-occupied with a busy lifestyle or not trust him because of previous experiences. My god-children are nearly all grown up and my relationships with them are even more special. Hannah lives an hour away so is much easier for me to see her when she wants to spend time with me, which is such a gift. These four children and the love we share has made my life complete. I can't have children now, but I don't feel I have missed out, because of these four. As for mum, well I still miss her every day, it's a pleasure to think of her rather than painful and I feel she is still with me – especially on the day I was married! Life will still have up's and downs but that's how you appreciate it. I have never been so calm and at peace!

Donna

SEPTEMBER 1st

# Take the opportunity today to consider The D.O.S.® Conversation.

Dan Sullivan the founder of the Strategic Coach®, one of the leading business coaching companies in the US, coined the term 'The D.O.S. Conversation®'.

That stands for:

**D**anger - What dangers do you have now that need to be eliminated?
**O**pportunities - What opportunities need to be captured?
**S**trengths - What strengths do you have that need to be maximised?

By asking these questions and analysing your replies you will gain deep insights into the options and opportunities in your life. Take some time to really try this. It might take an hour or two to actually give it the thought necessary - but the answers will be worth it.

Dangers might be job insecurity, or debt issues. Opportunities might be around learning new skills or connecting with likeminded people. Strengths might be your ability to network well or your organisational skills.

To learn more about Dan Sullivan and the Strategic Coach® Program go to: **www.StrategicCoach.com**

---

SEPTEMBER 2nd
# Take the opportunity today to write a letter to one of your children.

You may have children that are fully grown and living lives of their own. You may have teenagers still at home or in college. You may have younger children, maybe even toddlers or babies. Some of you might not have any children at all and others may have lost children.

Whichever situation you find yourself give this guide some thought. Something will come to mind. You may want to thank them. You may want to forgive them. You may want to apologise or simply reconnect. You may want to reminisce or encourage or send a simple message of love. You may want to speculate about what they may be like in years to come. You may want to beckon them.

Once written - post it. Maybe it'll have an address maybe it won't. But post it. That simple act will instantly embed that sentiment in your soul. It's not so important that your child reads it as much as you symbolically or actually send it. That letter will be a direct path into your emotions. Do it and see.

Incredible coincidence happened this evening. After I wrote this page I began some research on the net. It lead me to an interesting documentary about the great mathematician Georg Cantor. Although he ended up sadly in an institution he is now recognised as one of history's greatest thinkers. His motivation to continue despite countless peer criticisms throughout his life was a letter his father had written to him as a child, and which he carried with him all of his life. Wow! Incredible!

# Take the opportunity today to write down your achievements.

September 3rd is my mum's birthday. She passed away some years ago and I always remember on this day how inspirational she was. She always made me believe I could do anything if I set my mind to it. My dad did too, and between them I have always had a positive mindset.

Take time today to look back at what you've achieved in your life. Understand that at some time you probably thought those things would never happen - but they did. You achieved them.

Congratulate yourself then realise that what you might think is impossible right now, will one day be another one of your achievements. If you want it to be. If you are willing to work towards it with focus and determination.

SEPTEMBER 4th
# Take the opportunity today to ask 'What do I need to stop doing?'

Some things will spring to mind immediately - drinking, smoking, eating fatty foods etc. But other things may require some consideration. Procrastinating, distractability, negative thinking, blaming, judging, laziness and a million others.

Give it some thought and you'll identify those things that you *know* you need to stop. Discern if these traits are interfering with your level of fulfilment, happiness and satisfaction in life. You'll find they are. Now decide to stop them one by one.

It'll take effort - everything worthwhile does.

Believe me I have plenty of these. I'm working on them but every day requires effort. Some days I find myself slipping back but I take a breath, recognise what I'm doing - then stop. Sometimes Em helps me recognise them. (If you know what I mean!)  ;)

# Take the opportunity today to organise a party!

Sometimes we all need to let our hair down.

Have a party!

Even if you can't have one right away - organise and plan one. Just the act of planning will excite you.

In my youth I went to and had many parties. Some were a bit dull and some were fantastic. I was always excited about going and nearly always glad I went. If they were my parties then the clearing up was always a bit painful granted. If you end up having friends stay over at least you get help with that part.

Enjoy.

# Take the opportunity today to do some gardening - it will reconnect you to the source of everything.

Em's meditation is gardening. She potters about for hours, weeding, planting, harvesting. Then she comes in with a sedate smile on her face and a relaxed look all over.

It's not my thing, but here and there I do it. Of course I cut the lawn most weeks during summer but that's not really gardening. Even so, this simple task does give me half an hour in which to allow my mind to drift. I'm in the fresh air, I'm touching the ground.

Nurture the plants from time to time if you're not already a gardener and be aware of how it makes you feel.

SEPTEMBER 7th

# Take the opportunity today to STOP being resentful.

Resentment is a real joy killer. Yes it can act as a motivator in certain circumstances but why would you want it to be when you know there is no happiness or fulfilment in the outcome derived from it?

Resentment is blame in disguise. When we resent someone achieving something or winning something or getting something in any way, we are actually blaming something or someone for us *not* getting it.

"It's alright for them, they have..." is usually how our inner resentment will start our inner dialogue of excuses. Just be aware when you're doing it, allow it to run it's course for a minute or so, then smile, realise what it is and let it go. Now think of the opposite of what you were resentful about. If it was that someone is not helping you with something, think how helpful they are in other ways. This is usually enough to move you into a state of gratitude. Remember the mind can't be in two states at the same time.

I know this is harder than I make it sound, but have a go, practice it as often as you have resentful feelings.

# Take the opportunity today to turn a negative into a positive.

We all have negative experiences from time to time - hell, all of the time for some of us, right? Well they can become a bit overwhelming after a while as we replay some of the events in our minds over and over. I used to do this quite a bit, and still do to some degree. However, I have a strategy for limiting how frustrated or upset or angry I feel. I try and find the positive in the situation. I think it was Napoleon Hill that said: *"In every situation of adversity there is the seed for an equivalent or greater benefit."*

For instance me and Em just got back from a week holiday in Wales with the dogs. While we were there, we got lost finding the place, Em's mum had a mini stroke, one of the dogs got diarrhoea in the cottage at 4am and then on our only day to visit a nice town the dogs had a bark fest with such intensity and determination that we left after 20 minutes.

On the way home at the end of the week we decided that although the holiday was pretty much a wash-out we at least had some comical anecdotes to tell - which we have, to everyone we've met since getting back. We've had more fun telling those stories than we had on the actual holiday!

*"Seek and ye shall find."* - Matthew 7:7

Look for the positive in something and you <u>will</u> find it.

# Take the opportunity today to choose your friends wisely.

Those that scoff and are negative about your dreams will hold you back. You know the ones, it's possible they're your closest friends. Why do they do it? Partly because they don't want to see you fail, but partly because they don't want you to succeed. If you succeed there's a possibility you'll leave them behind. Not because you want to but because your life will lead you down different paths than before - paths which they will not be able to follow.

So, whilst you can't throw friendships away just because you become successful, consider carefully who's company you want to spend time in if you really do want to change your life. Good friends will be inspired by your success and may even model it to become successful themselves.

> **❝ A true friend never gets in your way unless you happen to be going down. ❞** - Arnold H. Glasgow

SEPTEMBER 10th

# Take the opportunity today to review your goals lists daily.

I read my 'A' Goals list every day but haven't been reading my 'B' or 'C' lists. I just did that and it took about two minutes! I think I'll be adding that to my daily routine.

Doing these daily tasks and making them a habit might not seem worthwhile at first but stick with it. As you make it a habit and you pay more attention to how you're feeling in the days, weeks and months ahead, I'm sure you'll start to notice a positive change. I certainly do, and as I don't know which of the daily routines has the most impact I just do them all. My life is way more positive and fulfilled than it used to be, so why would I stop?

> **66 Change requires stepping into uncertainty. 99**
>
> - Stuart Young

# Take the opportunity today to change your story.

I wonder how many excuses you use. You know the ones, where you give examples of why you're not further ahead in whatever area of your life you're talking about because...

'If only I'd done better at school.'

'If only we'd lived in such and such place we could have...'

'If only such and such had allowed us to...'

'If only my boss had...'

'If only the economy hadn't...'

etc. etc.

Time to change your story.

Believe me I had a story once (probably still do in some areas of my life) and it went kinda like this... *'If only my boss would just let <u>me</u> run this company it would be so much better.'* Followed closely by... *'If only he'd pay me what I'm worth.'* Which led on to *'If only I had my own clients I could do this myself.'*

Blah blah!

Eventually I changed my story, started my own company on a shoe string and ended up tripling my income in a two year period. So, get rid of your excuses, put your thinking cap on and start planning the life you want instead of moaning about the one you've got.

# Take the opportunity today to remember it's never too late.

Burt Goldman is about 84 years old (at the time of writing this). In his life he has travelled the world and studied under many masters of thought. He has an online community with hundreds of thousands of subscribers that turns over millions of dollars each year.

He is also an award winning photographer and prolific artist that sells his paintings for thousands of dollars each. He also plays the piano and writes his own music - well he is 84 after all, he's had a long time to achieve all these things.

Except...

He only started when he turned 80!

That's right, at the ripe old age of 80 Burt decided to turn his mind to achieving things he'd been thinking about for a long time but never got around to. Thankfully he had been training his *mind* for many decades and therefore knew how to apply himself to each goal.

Guess what? So can <u>You</u>.

That's right - it's never too late to learn something new or apply something you know. It just takes the desire to do so. So if one of your excuses is: '*it's too late for you*' - take a lesson from Burt, the moment you take your last breath is when it's actually too late.

To learn more about Burt Goldman go to:

**www.QuantumJumping.com**

SEPTEMBER 13th

# Take the opportunity today to eat only vegetarian food.

I used to be a massive meat eater. I would eat meat at least once or twice *a day*. Even now after being a vegetarian for a few years I can still appreciate the desire for a great peppered steak or venison stew.

The thing is it's pretty much undisputed now that eating too much meat really is bad for the human body. It's not used to it. The way we have evolved suggests for millennia we ate mainly fruit and vegetation with only the occasional meat or fish to supplement it. Many studies have proved that consuming too much red meat in particular leads to heart disease, cancer of one type or another and also promotes certain emotional issues such as hypertension and excessive anger.

On top of that we have now got to a stage where more land is set aside for producing meat products and the grain required to feed them than to agricultural land allocated for human consumption.

Give up meat, don't give up meat, decide for yourself but just for today give your body and the planet a day off.

*❝ Nothing will benefit human health and increase chances of survival of life on Earth as much as the evolution to a vegetarian diet ❞* - A. Einstein

SEPTEMBER 14th

# Take the opportunity today to pick up litter in your area.

You can do this on your own just to tidy your own local environment up a little or get involved in a local litter picking group. If there isn't one - <u>start one</u>!

This is how you get out there and make an immediate difference. This is how you meet like minded people. This is taking responsibility - where others haven't, ie: the litter bugs of the world.

Litter bugs are one of the banes of society, it shows a complete lack of respect and shows incredible levels of ignorance. Rather than moan about these under developed people become the example to them.

Your rewards will be way more than having a cleaner, tidier area to live in - believe me.

Went to my uncle's funeral today and it stirred some deep emotions inside me. The cemetery was beautifully kept even though many of the gravestones were dilapidated. I wish we afforded the same respect to our streets as we do to our cemeteries.

SEPTEMBER 15th

# Take the opportunity today to try Quantum Jumping.

Burt Goldman is the American Monk. He's in his 80s and having somewhat of a rennaisance in his career. He's never been so successful. (I mentioned his achievements just the other day.)

One of the techniques he has learned from his worldly travels is something he calls Quantum Jumping.

The idea is you do a short meditation and imagine you are travelling down a portal towards a doorway. When you go through the doorway you imagine you are in an alternate universe where the You of that place has achieved the thing that you desire in *this* universe.

You then converse with this other You to find out how they achieved it. This will help you tap into the hidden wisdom of your own subconscious or higher intelligence or indeed this alternate universe - whichever you want to believe.

Whatever way you want to view it, the results can be quite eye opening. Give it a go. Think of something you are struggling with at the moment then go find the You that's succeeded in doing that and ask them How.

Enjoy the experience - it may take a few attempts to get a clear vision.

To learn more about Burt Goldman and Quantum Jumping go to:
**www.QuantumJumping.com**

# Take the opportunity today to volunteer at a charity.

This is in the same vain as the litter picking from the other day. It's basically giving back to the community in some way, and one of the easiest and most rewarding ways is to volunteer at a local charity of your choosing.

Before considering this, get yourself into the mindset of being there for *them*. That is, setting your wants aside and what you want to get out of it and just giving them what *they* want or need.

You may have ideas of doing something really noticeable that will attract a lot of appreciation but when you get there they need help cleaning the toilets in the facility. If you can't find it within yourself to humbly take on that task with as much enthusiasm as you would in playing with the children, then think again. The point is to *help* them.

The opportunity to engage in those activities that are more suited to your skill sets and those that will have the greatest impact will emerge naturally.

If you think you're not ready to clean toilets I suggest you at least give it a try to be sure. If you discover you're not, then come back in a few months time. If you discover you are, then this will become an incredibly rewarding activity for you.

:)

# Take the opportunity today to write a thank you note to someone from your past.

If you sat and thought about those people that have had a major impact on your life you'd find there's probably only a handful. It may well be your parents or siblings. It may be a teacher or a neighbour. Maybe an uncle or cousin or simply the shopkeeper down the road.

Have a think, choose one, then write them a thank you note. Describe in detail the impact they have had on your life. Describe in as much detail as you can how your life is different because of their influence.

Then post that letter. It doesn't *have* to reach them, you may not know where they are now. They may not be with us anymore or you may not want them to read what you have written. Post it anyway. With just their name on the envelope if necessary. The symbolic gesture of dropping that letter in the post will be very therapeutic.

Now imagine how many people out there are thinking of You in this way. You can't know the full impact you've had on people because not all of them will share it with you. But you have.

# Take the opportunity today to sit with an elderly person and listen to their story.

All too often in our busy society our elderly are relegated to the corner of the room, patronised with one more cup of tea and humoured like children.

My uncle died recently, he was 92 and in the last few weeks of his life I was fortunate enough to have the time on a few occasions to visit him and my aunt in the home they were residing in for a while.

Each time I visited I made a point of asking some questions about their past and then sat and listened. There were some amazing stories that I'd never heard before and it was a privilege to hear them.

At his funeral one of his friends presented his eulogy and I learned that during World War II, when my uncle was in his early twenties, he was nearly killed by a bomb that demolished his in-law's house in London. Sadly his in-laws were both killed as was one of his young brother-in-laws. He managed to get himself and his young wife out of the wreckage then went back inside and dug his other 10 year old brother-in-law out of the rubble - saving his life. That young man was now the 82 year old vicar that was recounting this story at the graveside.

What an incredible story and I had to wait until he died before I heard it. Let's learn about the lives of our elderly from their own lips, we will be amazed and they will be thrilled.

# Take the opportunity today to bake some biscuits or a cake and give to a neighbour.

You ever had a neighbour come around to yours with a freshly baked cake or some biscuits? It's great isn't it? Even if you haven't, can you imagine how nice it would be?

Pass that on to someone else today - if you can't bake or don't have the time, buy a little pack of something from the shop and put them on your nicest plate and present them to a neighbour.

You'll brighten their day! (And your own.)

> *" Let's face it it, a nice creamy chocolate cake does a lot for a lot of people; it does for me! "*
>
> - Audrey Hepburn

# Take the opportunity today to Stop trying to help where it's not wanted.

Sometimes people aren't ready to be helped and you'll only frustrate yourself. We've all been there, trying to offer the right advice at the right time except it's being rejected.

You can see what's going on, it's obvious what needs to happen, you explain it clearly but your advice falls on deaf ears. Why is that?

Because the person you are trying to help is not *ready* to be helped. And you know what? We've all been in that place ourselves. If you really thought about it, you'd remember a time when you weren't ready for someone's help even though you knew it was the right thing. It may have been when you were a child and you were trying to ride your bike - you didn't want your dad holding you in case you fell, you wanted to do it on your own.

Although this is frustrating to the helper, sometimes it's exactly what's required as sometimes people have to just figure it out for themselves.

So, offer help but accept when it's not heeded.

---

Got a reminder of this just today. A friend mentioned they were unhappy with life at the moment. I asked if they wanted some help with that. I got an expletive filled reply that basically said I'd be the last person on earth they would take advice from. I wasn't even offering *my* help. I mentioned that, then wished them luck.

I'd be lying if I said it didn't wound me a little but I now know that's just my ego. No actual harm done - moved on.

---

# Take the opportunity today to look into someone's eyes for one minute without touching or talking.

Think it's easy?

Once you've stopped giggling and blinking, settle down to do it seriously. The whole giggling thing is our defence from someone getting too close. *Allow* them to get close because guess what - you're getting that close to *them*.

Be aware of your thoughts as you do this, notice if you are feeling more or less connected to that person. Notice if that person seems comfortable or awkward. Do you notice something *different* about them? Does your mind start to wander?

You are only as vulnerable as the person you are sharing this with. Having said that - you may find it really easy and enjoyable. I hope you do.

If you do find this quite easy, try doing it for two minutes or three.

:)

SEPTEMBER 22nd

# Take the opportunity today to consider who you ARE and not who you WERE.

Who we are, right now, is the residual product of our previous choices and decisions. That's who we *were* - 10 years ago, 5 years ago, last year, month week and even yesterday.

But today is a new day. Today you get to make new choices and decisions. Today you get to start afresh if you want with the opportunity of creating the You you want to be tomorrow, next week, next month, year etc.

Start this process by replaying the events of your day just before you go to sleep. Lie there and have them pan out exactly the way you wanted. Imagine all the events of the day happened *that way* in your favour.

Be aware of choices and decisions you made that didn't turn out how you wanted because you need to learn from them, but get excited by the imagining that even *they* are going to somehow turn to your advantage.

*❝ ...that the greatest waste in the world is the difference between what we are and what we could become. ❞*

- Ben Herbster

# Take the opportunity today to write down your top 20 frustrations with achieving your goals.

When I was taking Bob Proctor's Goal Achiever's Program my facilitator asked me to do this exercise. At first I thought it sounded a bit negative but I did it anyway - they know what they're talking about, right?

They did! It turned out to be a really powerful exercise.

Sitting down and really thinking about what is holding you back, articulating those frustrations and putting them in black and white for you to read will open your eyes.

Get them all out. If there's more than 20 that's ok - write them all. But do at least 20.

Start each one with the words: 'I'm frustrated that...'

I'm going to tell you tomorrow what to do next - no peeking!

Seriously, do this part first <u>BEFORE</u> looking at tomorrow's action.

To find out more about Bob Proctor visit: **www.BobProctor.com**

# Take the opportunity today to write the opposite of those frustrations from yesterday.

OK - this is where this exercise becomes really interesting and even more useful.

Let's say you wrote a frustration like this:
'I'm frustrated that I can't choose which goal to pursue first.'

The opposite would read something like:
'I understand fully which goal to pursue first.'

Now do that for every frustration you wrote.

Here's the next bit (and fun bit)...

... burn the first list of *actual* frustrations! Safely of course.
This symbolic gesture speaks to the unconscious mind. It says you don't value *those* ideas, so you're going to replace them (with the positive list), then destroy them.

Read your new list of affirming statements every day when you get up and last thing before you go to bed. The reason is, that is when you are either coming out of Alpha state or about to go into Alpha state. Alpha state is when you are most suggestible, so those new affirming statements are more likely to sink in.

I do this religiously now and each day I notice some more than others. They stand out more. They mean more. This is insight happening right in front of your own eyes. Do it - you'll see!

# Take the opportunity today to notice your surroundings.

We spend most our time virtually blind to our surroundings because we're immersed in them most days. Leave a book on the stairs for a few days and you stop noticing it's there. We get used to what we see every day and therefore have no need to *notice* it.

Now imagine you go to a new place, a holiday, a theatre, an open space. What do you do? You spend time taking it in. Absorbing the detail. Noticing the details. Exploring the experience of it all. It feels great doesn't it? It's how we enjoy, by noticing.

Spend today re-noticing your surroundings and you'll re-enjoy many aspects of it. We like enjoying things, we can enjoy more if we notice, so let's notice more often.

One other thing... when you take notice of your surroundings you may just get around to picking that flipping book off the stairs!

:)

# Take the opportunity today to follow a coincidence.

When you experience a coincidence ask yourself *why* you noticed it?

We've all got a different take on *what* a coincidence is.

Some think it's divine intervention. Some think it's luck. Some think it's just one of a million coincidences that are happening every day.

I believe in the last one but it doesn't matter which you believe. If you want to take something from it, if you want to make it a useful experience - ask the question above.

Find meaning in it. You may have to assign a meaning to it. Whatever, just find a meaning. Do that every time you experience a coincidence and you may find that those meanings start to add up to something.

# Take the opportunity today to remember the nicest thing you ever did for someone.

If you're a half way decent person you probably found that quite hard as you trawled through dozens of memories trying to find the nicest one.

I'll let you into a secret - that was actually the point!  :)

You see trying to figure out what the nicest thing was is impossible because you can't know how you have affected someone when you do something nice. At the time they might just say 'Oh, thanks for that.' and you don't hear any more, but unbeknownst to you that thing turns out on reflection to be massively influential for that person. So what you think is the nicest thing may well be pretty good, but it might pale in comparison to something else you did that seemed quite small.

So the point of the guide?

Do nice things all the time no matter how small they are because you don't know the long term effects of that action.

> **" As the butterfly beats its wings and causes a hurricane, so every life has an effect beyond its comprehension. "** - Stuart Young

# Take the opportunity today to remember the nicest thing someone ever did for You.

This might get your brain box going or you may be a very fortunate person and have a plethora of memories. Whichever, remember the occasion, remember where you were, what you were doing, then what did someone do. Now recall how you felt about it. If it stuck with you it must have made quite an impression. Enjoy remembering every detail about that experience.

Now send a thank you message to that person reminding them just how their action affected you. Send a letter or an email or a text or a video of yourself saying thanks.

Finally, think about how you might be able to do something really nice for someone else. Think of how it may make *them* feel.

:)

# Take the opportunity today to Reuse something.

The three 'R's of the sustainable world are: <u>Reduce, Reuse, Recycle.</u>

Today look around you and think what you or someone else might be able to Reuse. In fact do not throw anything away today without considering how it might be Reused in some way. Do this often and before you know it you'll habitually think of how to Reuse stuff and you'll have helped the planet in some small way.

Why not offer it for free on: **Freecycle.com**

Or,

Get some money for it by offering it for a nominal price on: **Preloved.com**

SEPTEMBER 30th

# Take the opportunity today to review the guides of this month to see which ones you may have missed.

If you're still with me so far pat yourself on the back as we're three quarters through the year now, and I sincerely hope you have noticed some changes in your life since starting to read this book and implement it's guides. Keep going over this month's guides as often as you can to give yourself the best chance of noticing one that will grab your attention. It's those guides that grab you that you should put most effort into doing. There are literally hundreds in this book so I'm 100% certain many will prove useful, inspirational, motivational and ultimately life changing.

---

Make a note in your journal or diary of any changes you have noticed since you started this book.

---

# Take the opportunity today to try the Inner Chamber technique.

David & Kristin Morelli, creators of one of the top 5 iTunes podcasts - *'Energy Is Everything'* are big believers in the use of intuition. In order to tap into your intuition on a regular basis they came up with a formula - they call it the Inner Chamber technique.

There's a few simple things to remember before you start which are: you have to be sincere, be willing to listen, be open, have no expectations and have a clear question or intention ready.

Here's a summary of the technique:

Think of a question you would like to investigate. Craft it well.

Start by sitting in a quiet place and relax for a few minutes.

Take a few deep breaths and bring your awareness completely to where you are.

Then imagine you slip wonderfully down a tube-slide and you end up at a door. Notice how the door looks, every detail.

Open the door and enter the chamber, look around and notice how it looks and how you feel inside - this is your private place.

Go to the centre of the chamber and then when you feel relaxed and ready, ask your question.

Listen. Take a mental note of the answers that come.

Take those answers a bit deeper if necessary by asking 'What does that mean?'

When you're ready, take a few more deep breaths and allow yourself to come back to where you are right now.

Now let the answers simmer. Make some notes about those answers.

Finally, when you understand the answers you received - take some action.

It may take you a few times to really start getting some useful information but keep trying. When it happens you will feel exhilarated!

To find out more about David & Kristin Morelli go to:

**www.EverythingIsEnergy.com**

# Take the opportunity today to notice where you might be self-sabotaging.

Following on from yesterday's guide I thought I'd share another one of David & Kristin Morelli's techniques, this time it's about self-sabotage and how we can spot it.

The crux of it is the idea that we all have a preferred energy level. Whether you are feeling a bit low so you seek out some excitement or on a high so seek out an argument, both are utilised to reset our energy level back to the preferred setting.

Have you ever been on a real high after getting a raise from your boss or getting a date with a hot person or maybe you just had a great time with some friends, then you find yourself getting in to some silly row over something with a loved one? If that rings a bell give some thought to what your button is. What's your trigger? Fear? Anxiety? Guilt? Look and you'll find it, then next time you can anticipate it ahead of time and maybe even nip it in the bud.

# Take the opportunity today to take a nap if you need it.

There is a lot of scientific evidence to support the notion that napping is actually a highly beneficial pursuit.

The important aspect of napping is to get the timing right. The most important part of any sleep period is dreaming. If you don't get a chance to dream you will not feel any benefit from the sleep. So your goal with napping is to get into REM state (Rapid Eye Movement ie: Dreaming) as quickly as possible. Then, wake up as soon as possible once it has passed. If you allow yourself to go into deeper sleep you will find it very hard to wake and will feel groggy and tired.

So how do you do that?

Thankfully tests have shown that most people will need between 15 and 30 minutes of sleep to experience REM, so start with that. You'll have to experiment with an alarm clock to find your optimum time but once you find it you'll find you can wake feeling refreshed and alert.

Lastly for anyone who thinks napping is for kids, the elderly and sherkers - here's a handful of famous nappers: Richard Branson, Bill Clinton, Winston Churchill and Leonardo da Vinci - so you'll be in good company.

OCTOBER 4th

# Take the opportunity today to write down 10 achievements you're happy with in your life.

Every now and then we all need reminding of just how far we've come. What we've achieved, where we've been, what we've done and who we've shared it all with.

If you're one of those people that think that your life has been a waste up till now, do this exercise as soon as possible. No need to stop at 10 either. When you've finished, read the list aloud and be proud of who you are. Now consider what you still can do, be, have, experience etc.

There's a whole lot of life out there - go get some!

:)

> " *If we all did the things we were capable of doing, we would literally astound ourselves.* "
>
> - Thomas Edison

OCTOBER 5th
# Take the opportunity today to plant something.

I think I've already mentioned that I'm no gardener. I leave that to Em, she's good at it and she loves it. But every so often I like to plant stuff. A couple of years ago Em bought me one of those shallow barrels - you know the ones, they look like cut down old fashioned beer kegs. Well, I wanted to have a tiny bit of the garden just for me, just to plant the things I like. So that's what I did. We went and bought some flowers that I liked the look of and I planted the whole barrel up. I'm not sure what plants are good to put in the ground in October but I'm sure there are some. I could blurb on about how you're nurturing life and creating beauty or something like that and it'd be true. But to be honest I don't know exactly why it feels good to do - it just does. That's obviously why Em and other avid gardeners are out there all the time. Me, I like to do it here and there. When the feeling grabs me.

I hope the feeling grabs you.

Just took a look at my barrel tucked away in one corner of our patio. It looks a bit neglected so I'll go ask Em what I can plant in it. She might say I have to wait till spring. I hope not.

# Take the opportunity today to entertain some kids by being daft.

Is there anything more fun than goofing around with some kids. As we grow older we run the risk of forgetting how enjoyable it is to just run around making a lot of noise and being daft. Watch some kids playing, you won't find them feeling self conscious - that's the disease of the grown up.

A word of warning; if the kids you're thinking of being daft with aren't your own - as the sergeant used to say in Hill Street Blues: *"Let's be careful out there."* It goes without saying, but make sure you know them and make sure they're happy for you to join in. You don't want to freak them out! (Or their parents.)

;)

OCTOBER 7th
# Take the opportunity today to accept.

Accept what?

Well, everything! Accept that you woke up late and will now get a lecture from your boss. Accept that the economy is making it harder to make ends meet. Accept that your team aren't going to win the league, or competition, or game. Accept that you might have to learn new skills in order for you to reach your goals. Accept that the person you're crazy about pays you no attention. Accept that your childhood wasn't as great as some people you know. Accept that you weren't born with a silver spoon in your mouth. Accept that you *were* born with a silver spoon in your mouth. Accept that you may not be able to run the fastest, jump the highest, throw the furthest.

Accepting doesn't mean you can't change things. It means sometimes things *won't* change and you have to be ok with that. When something is unchangeable and you don't accept it, it'll eat away at you until there's nothing left.

When you get to a place of acceptance you will feel a whole lot more relaxed. A whole lot less frustrated, angry or helpless. You will feel a huge weight lift off your shoulders. So look at your circumstances today and consider what you can accept.

> **Life can either be accepted or changed. If it is not accepted, it must be changed. If it cannot be changed, then it must be accepted.** - Unknown

OCTOBER 8th

# Take the opportunity today to notice any aches or pains - then let them go.

This is not some magic trick although I will give you an exercise you can do to *actually* reduce your aches and pains. No, this is about letting go of the suffering of pain. Pain is a part of life but suffering is optional - Anthony Robbins said that and I agree with him 100%. When you experience physical pain it is your body trying to communicate where you need to take care. So listen, but don't become a slave to it. OK so you can't pick up stuff the way you used to, find another way or pick up less. OK so that broken bone is throbbing like a SOB, of course it is - it's *mending*.

Stop moaning and groaning about the aches and pains you have, they're valid I know, but it's not helping you. Let them go.
Say: '*OK, it hurts, I'll work around it till it doesn't.*' Beat that pain into submission. So, on to the trick.

If you have some binoculars or can borrow some, look at that part of your body that is aching or in pain using the wrong end - so things look smaller. If it's your finger just hold it out in front of you and using the wrong end of the binoculars look at it. It'll seem farther away and your brain actually connects the image with the feeling and the pain reduces. You may need to use a mirror if it's your shoulder or head etc. Try it and see.

> I read about this recently in an NLP book and apparently studies show most people feel a significant reduction in perceived pain. I tried it on my frozen shoulder and I think it has made a difference. You have to do it for a while - I've done it every evening for about four weeks.

318

OCTOBER 9th

# Take the opportunity today to ask yourself a positive question.

Burt Goldman suggests this process as a way of staying positive. If for instance you were to ask yourself: *'Why don't I quit smoking?'* that would be negative. Your mind will actually go off and try and answer the question and it will find reasons, such as: *'Because I like it.'* or *'Because it relaxes me.'* This then convinces you to continue.

If however, you rephrase the question: *'What would my life be like if I quit smoking?'* then your mind will find answers to that request, such as: *'I'd feel better in the morning.'* or *'This damn cough would go away.'* or *'I could play with the kids without getting wheezy after two minutes.'* etc.

Next time you're asking yourself something, try this process and see how different you feel.

OCTOBER 10th

# Take the opportunity today to be daft for your own amusement. :)

The other day I suggested that you be daft with some kids, today I suggest you do it just for yourself. You might want to do it right where you are in the office or the coffee shop or on the street, or you might want to wait until you're on your own. Whichever makes you feel most comfortable.

Now remember when you were a kid and you used to make funny noises or you'd get a burst of excess energy and you'd have to run around pretending you were a fighter jet or riding a horse? Do that now or any other thing that takes your fancy. Make it ridiculous. Make it nonsensical. But make it fun and exhilarating.

Go on, you know you want to. :)

I do this all the time, so I know what I'm talking about. :)

OCTOBER 11th

# Take the opportunity today to make yourself a cuppa then just sit and enjoy it. :)

I'm looking forward to doing this today. How often do you really enjoy a good cup of tea or coffee? If you're anything like me then you usually have a cup on the go, while you're checking your emails, or reading the paper, or washing the car, or doing the hoovering - you get the idea.

Today I will be taking ten minutes to just sit with a cuppa. I'm going to call it my TWIP time - Think, Wonder, Imagine and Ponder.

You?

Wow! I'm surprised at just how excellent that was. I just took ten minutes and sat with a cuppa. Nothing else. My mind just started wandering all over the place. I felt really relaxed and calm and that's when the ideas started coming. One then two, three and so on until it was like an avalanche. In the end I drained my mug and ran up to my office to enter this and make a bunch of notes about the ideas.
I think I'm going to have to make a habit of that! :)

# Take the opportunity today to get in touch with your envy.

Most people are envious in some way or another of someone else. We love the house they live in or the car they drive or the partner they're with or the lifestyle they lead yada yada.

Then the guilt button might go on. Often people feel bad for feeling envious. There's no need. Envy can be a good thing. Envy drives us on to create the same in *our* lives. Envy can be the fuel you need to reach your goals. Envy can be useful.

Jealousy however is envy's darker sibling. Jealousy wants what someone else *has*. Not something the same or similar but *actually* what they have. Jealousy leads to lies and deceit and resentment. In the worst cases it can lead to hate, anger and crime.

So the next time you want what someone else has consider whether you are being jealous or envious. If it's the latter, allow that to spur you on to get the same. Use what they have as a model. Even go as far as to ask them how they got what it is you want.

Good luck.

# Take the opportunity today to understand your dissatisfaction.

Bob Proctor of The Secret says that we should always be happy but never satisfied. It's our dissatisfaction that drives us to change things, to think of improvements, to make progress. For instance you can be happy with the car you drive but still strive to find a more economical, environmental, faster, more comfortable version. You pick the improvement! If you own the latest Ferrari you might think it's perfect but I bet you'd like to get 200 miles to the gallon - especially when you're driving at 100mph (on a private track of course!).

So next time you feel dissatisfied, welcome the feeling and discern what it's trying to tell you. Consider what improvements need to be made in that area. Use it as a motivator.

# Take the opportunity today to act as if.

Remember when you were a kid and you acted as if you were a cowboy or a ballet dancer or a racecar driver or a princess? You really got into the part didn't you? You lived the part as if you were that person. The fun was that while you *acted as if,* you actually felt that way. It felt good, hell, it felt great!

Trouble is as we grow up we are conditioned to stop acting and start behaving. Behaving this way or that way and the *acting as if* gets drummed out of us. The thing is *acting as if* is a creative process, it gets your subconscious mind thinking about how to make that acting <u>real</u>. It starts to offer suggestions about how that acting could be true. It offers evidence that that acting could *be.*

So I suggest today you *act as if* you <u>are</u> who you really want to <u>be</u>. Then see what comes out of it.

*Acting as if* is also integral to most visualisation techniques. When considering your goals you should *act as if* you have already attained them.

OCTOBER 15th

# Take the opportunity today to 'scramble' a bad memory.

One of Tony Robbins' many psychological techniques is the NAC (Neuro Associative Conditioning) Process. One of those techniques deals with bad memories. He refers to it as '*scrambling*'.

The process is supposed to rewire that memory so that it no longer gives you the bad feelings associated with it.

The idea is you rerun the bad memory as if it were a film. Imagine seeing it from different angles, edit it so it seems like you're watching it on a cinema screen. Then change the characters in the memory to cartoons, including yourself. Run the memory forwards and then backwards. Do this over and over a few times speeding it up as you do so. Then change the colours of the faces to rainbows and add some comical music.

Have the antagonist in the scene go crosseyed and have a speech bubble above their head filled with the words '*Blah, blah, blah!*'

Do this and your neural pathways connected with that memory will become scrambled and it'll be almost impossible to remember that experience the same way ever again.

If you have some memories that play in your mind over and over, giving you feelings you'd rather not have, have a go at this. It might take a few attempts but it'll be worth it.

To learn more about the incredible Tony Robbins and his distinct style of Life Coaching go to: **www.TonyRobbins.com**

# Take the opportunity today to let go of any grudge you feel.

Do you hold any grudges? Think about that for a moment. A grudge *can* lay hidden, sometimes for years. Think for a moment.

If you have found one, think about the person you hold that grudge against. Notice how you feel as you imagine their face. Feel that hurt - just for a moment.

Now imagine that person as a child. See them playing, running, laughing. See them falling and hurting their knee. Imagine you go to that child and you ease their pain, comfort their tears. You help them to their feet. You rub their hurt knee.

Imagine they stop crying and return to playing. See if the feelings you had about that person have changed at all.

There is a small child in every one of us.

OCTOBER 17th

# Take the opportunity today to get rid of something from your house you don't need.

Most people have stuff in their house that if it went missing they'd never notice. Ask yourself why do you still hold on to it then. OK, photos and letters and important documents get filed away - but we're not talking about them. We're talking about things that really serve no purpose, have no value (to you), are never going to be used again - you get the idea.

If yours is anything like my house you even have someone telling you to get rid of certain stuff, right? So, do it! Bite the bullet and move stuff on, give it a new home or give it a welcome send off.

You'll feel better for it - eventually if not immediately!

And before you think it, yes - five minutes after you've got rid of whatever it is, you'll need it. For the first time in five years! So what, get over it! That's how it works. :)

OCTOBER 18th

# Take the opportunity today to ask *who* you admire and *why*.

Everyone admires someone. It might be somebody famous, a great athlete or celebrity for instance, it might be someone from history or an outstanding person in your community. It might even be someone very close to you.

Once you identify *who* that is, ask *why* that is.

The why should give you a good idea of what you want to be more like. This is why you admire them after all. Think of how you might be able to model their behaviour. In what ways could you be more like them?

Now - try and be like that.

OCTOBER 19th

# Take the opportunity today to notice when you're comparing yourself to others - then STOP!

Unlike yesterday's guide which was about identifying traits in some-one you admire so that you can figure out how you can be more like them, today's guide tries to address needless comparisons.

Have you ever thought that someone else was prettier than you, cleverer than you, earned more money than you? These are the pointless comparisons which will only leave you feeling inadequate. Yesterday's guide should have inspired you. The above kind of com-parison will only bring you down.

On the other hand envy can be a motivational force. If you like the house someone lives in or the car they drive or the type of work they do, all of these things can help you aspire to have those things too.

All I'm saying is discern if you are being motivated to emulate or whether you are becoming depressed by thinking you're not good enough.

If it's the latter - STOP!

# Take the opportunity today to write a list of things that you are afraid of.

For some this will be a short list and others it will be longer than it should. I for one am afraid of dying before I achieve a lot more than I have right now for instance. But give it some real thought, take a bit of time over it and write down everything that comes to mind.

It may surprise you just how long or short it actually is.

It's funny how identifying our fears can actually diminish them. Once your list is complete, read it a few times. Notice how you feel about each item. You may feel some are silly, others irrelevant.

This execise in itself may spur you on to tackle some of those fears, some of which you may only *think* you have. We define ourselves in many ways and one way is through our fears - I'm afraid of heights, or spiders, or flying, or open spaces etc. Thing is, you *may* have been afraid once but that doesn't necessarily mean you *still* are.

# Take the opportunity today to write the opposite of being afraid.

Yesterday I asked you to write a list of things you were afraid of and today I want you to try and write the opposite of that list.

For instance the opposite of my fear of dying before I achieve much more might be: I am confident that I will achieve everything I wish to well before I die.

This might take a bit longer than the first list, due to you navigating the words needed to turn it into the opposite. Spend the time though.

Done it?

Good, now burn the previous *afraid* list.

Why?

Because symbolically you are telling your subconscious that *that* list is unimportant, that in fact it doesn't even exist.

# Take the opportunity today to ignore any negative comments you hear.

Do you have people in your life that are just totally negative about everything you do? OK, maybe not *everything*, but quite a lot of things? Hmm, you must learn to let those comments wash over you. Those people may wish you the best, they may even love you, but they don't know your strength, your resilience or your perseverance. Hell, you might not even know those things about yourself - but they are there.

So, avoid those negative people that you can and ignore the negative comments of the ones you can't. Just say in your mind 'They don't know me' every time they bring you down with words like:

'*...be realistic...*' or

'*...you're no good at that...*' or

'*...I don't think that's your strength...*' etc.

As you learn to do this you will start to believe in yourself more and more. It's a good feeling.

OCTOBER 23rd

# Take the opportunity today to chunk down.

Chunking down (or up for that matter) is a psychological process used in hypnotherapy and NLP to help get specific about a certain issue.

An example conversation might be something like this:

Q: 'So, why are you feeling angry today?'

A: 'Because my boss keeps criticising my work.'

Q: 'Why does that make you feel angry?'

A: 'Because there's nothing wrong with my work.'

Q: 'So why does that make you feel angry?'

A: 'Because it feels like he's picking on me.'

Q: 'And why does that make you feel angry?'

A: 'Because I'm worried that I might get fired.'

Q: 'And why would that make you feel angry?'

A: 'If I got fired I couldn't pay my mortgage etc.'

Q: 'Why would that make you feel angry?'

A: 'Because I don't like feeling uncertain about stuff like that.'

Q: 'So why does being uncertain make you feel angry?'

A: 'Because my family depends on me.'

Q: 'Does your family depending on you make you feel angry?'

A: 'Yes, it puts pressure on me.'

You see from this simple example how a critical boss is blamed for the pressure someone might feel from family obligations - that might not actually be real. From here a discussion with the family could ensue to find out if there really is this dependency.

Good NLP books will deal with chunking in more depth.

OCTOBER 24th

# Take the opportunity today to chunk up.

*Chunking Down* helps you get specific, but *Chunking Up* helps you see the bigger picture. Both are useful techniques to help individuals get clearer about certain issues, but chunking can be a highly productive negotiation process. Using Chunking Up one can get multiple parties to get agreement about common objectives whilst Chunking Down to find the details of the agreement.

An individual conversation might be something like this:

Q: 'Why do you want to write a book?'

A: 'Because I find it exciting.'

Q: 'What's exciting about it?'

A: 'That I'm creating something completely new.'

Q: 'And why would that be exciting to you?'

A: 'I like the idea of other people getting enjoyment from my book.'

Q: 'Why is it important that other people enjoy it?'

A: 'Because if a lot of people enjoyed it I could earn a lot of money.'

Q: 'And why would a lot of money be exciting to you?'

A: 'Because I would be free to write more books.'

Q: 'And would you get more enjoyment from getting even more money?'

A: 'Of course, but the thought of people liking my work is more important.'

Q: 'More important than the money?'

A: 'Equally, I think! It would be great for thousands of people to like me and think I was creative.'

Hmm, I think I'm finding out something about myself here!! :)

# Take the opportunity today to accept your mistakes.

Fortunately for me I've never made a mistake in my life!

Yeah right!

It's a bit of a cliché to say we must learn from our mistakes but here's the thing - if you become afraid of mistakes you take less risks. If you take less risks it means pushing yourself less. If you push yourself less you'll achieve less, get less, experience less and ultimately, live less of a life.

Not all of us are bungee jumping, skydiving, white-water-rafting thrill seekers, but, we each have to find our own risk limits. One of those bungee jumpers may be terrified of starting their own company for instance. So, find your comfort zone, then step outside it a little. Then a little bit more and so on. When you make a mistake, retrace your steps, find where you went wrong, apply an amended strategy and go again.

Mistakes are our teachers - look forward to meeting them, embrace them, then suck every ounce of wisdom out of them as you can.


:)

OCTOBER 26th

# Take the opportunity today to accept your friend's mistakes.

Some find it even harder to accept mistakes their friends make than they do their own. Especially when it's personal, it can feel like inconsideration at least, betrayal at worst. Take a moment to think about letting go of your own mistakes, mistakes you may have made that upset someone close to <u>you</u>. Were you forgiven, did you want to be forgiven but weren't? How did it make you feel?

See if you can use those feelings of wanting to make it up to that person and apply them to your friend when they have upset *you*. We're all just doing the best from where we are in our lives and sometimes that's not very good. We all deserve another chance though.

OCTOBER 27th

# Take the opportunity today to start a philosophers club.

Every tuesday night I go training and have done for many years. Afterwards the handful of members go down the pub for a pint and a chat. Some time after this had been going on we found that most of our conversations were pretty deep and meaningful (as meaningful as a bunch of blokes can get that is).

Eventually we branded the pub gathering 'The Philosophers Club'.

Over the years we have had many many great conversations ranging from the social ills of the world, the economy, war, life and death and the hereafter. We now look forward to 'The Philosophers Club' as much as we look forward to the training.

This is a mind expanding experience especially if you have members from all walks of life with differing opinions. Think about starting one today. You'll engage with others as well as engaging with yourself. This is a great opportunity to change other people's minds and for them to change yours.

# Take the opportunity today to trust.

Be open. Be transparent. Tackle issues head-on. Be discerning about how much 'character trust' and 'competence trust' you *give*.

1. How much integrity do those around you have and do you have? and

2. How competent in getting the job done are they or you?

Without trust we could not function in society. We have to trust that other drivers on the road will not run into us for the hell of it. We have to trust that the doctor at the hospital knows how to heal us. We have to trust the justice system is protecting us. We have to trust that those close to us are being honest and loyal.

A lack of basic trust will make us paranoid, I imagine a lot of conspiracy theorists have very low levels of trust. Of course, we have to remain vigilant to the truth, you can't believe all you read or hear on the news. Advertising and election campaigns can be misleading at best.

But keep a healthy level of trust and *accept* that it'll be misplaced at times.

> *" See, when you make a commitment you build hope. When you keep a commitment you build trust. "*
>
> - Stephen M. R. Covey

# Take the opportunity today to be mindful - stare at something for 10 minutes.

Today's exercise is all about how to stay focused on your goals using Mindfulness.

Mindfulness is a mental strategy that allows you to be aware of your 'state' of mind at any given time and a tactic to control that state.

The idea is that when you feel a bit down or demotivated or confused etc. you can spiral downwards into those negative thoughts if you're not careful. By observing that you're in a negative state you can then decide to choose a positive state instead. One of inspiration, motivation and focus.

If you're able to do this at will you can spiral upwards instead of downwards and therefore remain on track more easily.

Using Mindfulness you can learn to stay more positive for much longer and get much more done.

So, here's the simplest way of being Mindful that I've experienced and it can be done anywhere, anytime:

1. Sit down somewhere reasonably quiet
2. Choose something to focus your attention on (anything in a fixed position will do) - your vision board if you've done one, if you're at home at the time
3. Focus all of your attention on that thing for 10 minutes
4. Notice everything about that thing, wonder about how big it is 'exactly', wonder how it was made, notice it's colours and

textures - put ALL of your attention on THAT thing!

5. As your attention drifts to other objects or thoughts, gently bring yourself back to that object you are focusing on.

This exercise repeated as often as you can will train your mind to focus on what YOU want to focus on. Remember what you focus on becomes what you attract, so your vision board is a good place to start. It will help you tune out distractions on the outside and on the inside.

When you do it for the first few times you'll find yourself easily distracted and 10 minutes will feel like an hour! KEEP PRACTISING!

This is powerful so I urge you to take the time to do it - I started with watching a candle flame just before bedtime. Trouble is if you want to do it during the day that becomes a bit difficult.

Enjoy this process.


NOTE: As you become more proficient at this you'll start to notice some of the thoughts that are distracting you are actually making a lot of sense. They might be answering questions you have about projects on the go or relationship issues etc. Start to notice these and take notes about them before getting back to your Mindfulness. These are Golden Nuggets of wisdom coming through your subconscious. Not every distraction is junk! :)

# Take the opportunity today to make something.

I find that the act of making something can either be so absorbing that the clutter of daily thoughts fades into the background, or, making that thing is so automatic that your mind can drift away almost like meditating.

Whichever experience you have it will be valuable, plus you end up with something at the end of it. Maybe it's dinner! Maybe it's a painting or a sculpture, or a textile object. Whatever it is it's therapeutic to *make* it. It didn't exist until you created it. That in itself is worth doing it for.

OCTOBER 31st

# Take the opportunity today to review the guides of this month to see which ones you may have missed.

Well done for getting this far and I sincerely hope you have noticed some changes in your life since starting to read this book and implement it's guides. Keep going over this month's guides as often as you can to give yourself the best chance of noticing one that will grab your attention. It's those guides that grab you that you should put most effort into doing. There are literally hundreds in this book so I'm 100% certain many will prove useful, inspirational, motivational and ultimately life changing.

---

Make a note in your journal or diary of any changes you have noticed since you started this book.

---

CASE STUDY 5

# Vicky's Story

A few years ago life was dull, I suppose that is the best way to describe it.

I love my husband and both children dearly but back then I lacked any motivation. I took the kids to school, went to work, picked the kids up from school, chatted to the other mothers in the playground about things that mothers talk about. Took the kids to their various activities with the help of my husband, Colin, and looked forward every day to that first glass of wine once he was home. Stuart would often join us and we would put the world to rights, but we would often talk about people's out-look on life and how it affected what was going on in their lives.

I had suffered from post natal depression with both of my children and had an interest in bringing them up with a positive view point. Colin and I decided that we would show the kids *how* to do things safely rather than stopping them doing something. So, we taught them *how* to climb trees rather than just warning them to be care-ful while they were trying. I was confident that this was the way to bring my children up but I didn't stop to think that the same princi-ples could apply to me. That if I looked after *me* and did things that I enjoyed this would make me a better mother and wife and I would be much happier doing it.

During one of our 'relax with a glass of wine evenings' Stuart was telling us about this film he had watched, he was so enthusiastic about it, it was unreal, so we (I have to admit after about a week) found it on the internet and watched it. That film changed my life.

I started realising that I was right in my attitude to bringing my children up and was starting to see how things really worked. From that moment on things slowly started making sense.

Now, I LOVE a bargain (as Stuart and my husband will both tell you), and I started noticing that when I was going shopping I would think *'Oh I'd really like...'* and there it would be. I still use this process every time I'm looking for something. (My son has also mastered it to a tee.) Only the other week I wanted a pair of navy blue shoes. I went to my favourite shoe shop. No Navy, not this season's colour. I checked the sale rail - navy with white stitching, not my size. I decided I'll just see if there's another pair put back in the wrong place, so I went to the stand - I spotted exactly what I was looking for, oh no, they were two sizes too small - that's what the label said, only I thought hang on they don't look like a size six, so I turned them over to look on the bottom and there it was, a size eight and a perfect fit and 50% off - that's The Secret for you!

The Year that I first watched The Secret was the year of my 40th birthday and Rhonda Byrne had just released her first book of the same title. I received it as one of my most precious presents and this book is in my life to stay. I have lent it to friends to share the knowledge but they are always aware just how special it is to me and it is always returned.

I read and pondered this book and looked at my personality, that summer we went on our family holiday to France. Warm weather and good wine, only I realised after reading a book on drinking, that I no longer wanted to drink alcohol and that I didn't need it to relax and enjoy myself. I started looking at other positive ways of doing things. I decided to not drink anything on that holiday and to see how things changed. It wasn't difficult as I now had a strong attitude to it, I didn't need anyone to support me in the process because I had the confidence in my self to do it on my own. I realised that in actual fact it was easier not to drink than it was to have a glass of wine and restrict myself to one or two. Some of my friends still comment now on how they can't believe I've done it, but do you know what, it wasn't difficult. I realised a couple of years later that I don't actually like the taste of it. I mistakenly picked my friend's glass of Rosé up one time and could hear them all laughing at me as I ran to the kitchen sink to spit it out!

Now I always focus on the positive, I know that if I think positively then good things will happen. I like *not* always knowing what they're going to be, as I enjoy the surprise. I have had the confidence to decide to try different roles out in the organisation I work for, some I haven't enjoyed and have tested my belief, but I have carried on focusing on the positive and believed that if I wasn't enjoying something that was because the universe was sorting out something better. And it has, I lie in bed every night now and am grateful for my day, I say thank you for all the good things that have happened, (even if my teenage kids haven't seen it that way). I am not perfect, but my life *is*, everything happens for a reason.

Even though I have had a very challenging time at work recently, I love my job and my family. Colin has helped out with a particular project that I've been working on and as a 'thanks', my boss sent me a text the other night - it reads (and I will never delete it!) *'You should be so proud, you have a lovely husband and family plus you can turn your hand to all this work.'* And do you know what, I am!

Vicky

NOVEMBER 1st

# Take the opportunity today to practise letting go.

Hale Dwoskin's The Sedona Method, is a process of eliminating negative emotions by using a simple 5 step process. For instance, remember a time when you felt really angry (or some other negative emotion). Imagine the occurrence or circumstance you were in when you felt that emotion. Then ask yourself:

1. 'Can I allow and welcome my [anger] to be here?' then ask:

2. 'Can I release or let go of this [anger]?

In the first two questions you are searching for permission to feel that emotion. Anger for instance, can be helpful. However, if you drill down into that feeling you might find that your anger makes you feel protected, strong or right about something. Delve into those feelings. Do they serve you? Maybe yes, maybe no. Either way, feelings are natural and should not be suppressed. Now you've got a hold of that emotion and are experiencing it in a controlled way, you can move on to examining the next questions:

3. 'Would I let it go?' then,

4. 'When?'

These next two questions are designed to allow you to properly consider whether you can live without those feelings about that circumstance. When you realise that you are in control of holding on or letting go - *decide* to let go.

The fifth step of the process is to Repeat the first four steps with any and every negative emotion you feel. As you become practiced at it you will be able to apply it while you actually feel negative emotions in the future - as they occur.

For more info and a trailer for the film go to: **www.LettingGo.tv**

NOVEMBER 2nd

# Take the opportunity today to let go of any hate you feel.

Hopefully you got the chance to have a go at this letting go process yesterday. Now try it with any hate you may feel. Sometimes we have feelings of hate towards people that have hurt us in the past, sometimes we feel hate towards people in power and we often feel hate towards those we don't understand and maybe frighten us. Terrorists for example can rouse a good level of hate amongst many people. Immigrants are another group who inspire hate amongst many.

As you practise the process of letting go, you will become clearer about *why* you have the feelings you have. Hopefully this will be a revealing experience. One that will give you a deeper understanding of yourself, your thoughts and your behaviour.

> **" When you let go you feel like you're falling when in fact you are flying. "**
>
> - Stuart Young

# Take the opportunity today to let go of any feelings of inadequacy.

Following on from the letting go theme of the last couple of days I thought I'd explore some other less identifiable emotions. When you are feeling inadequate for example, it can often manifest as anger or shame or of being victimised. Be sure as you apply this process that you delve into the *why* of your feelings. More often than not a different emotion lurks beneath the surface of another.

> **" Compassion is NOT created as a result of conditions, certain conditions are created as a RESULT of compassion. "**
>
> -Neale Donald Walsch

NOVEMBER 4th

# Take the opportunity today to let go of any jealousy you are feeling.

This process is so powerful I thought I'd dwell on it a while longer. The more you use it the easier it becomes and the more likely you are to experience a breakthrough. When you can get to the point of allowing a negative emotion to dissipate until it is no longer discernable you have successfully let go of it. That's not to say continual practise is not necessary - it is! The more you do it the better you'll become and before you know it life will just seem easier, more joyful and relaxing.

Try it with jealousy. I used to find it difficult to tell the difference between jealousy and envy until I used a technique that gave me clarity. Envy means wanting the *same* as someone else, whereas jealousy means wishing to *deprive* someone of what they have so you can have it instead.

## NOVEMBER 5th

# Take the opportunity today to let go of any anger you feel.

If when you tried the Sedona Method the first time you chose something other than anger - try it with anger now. Anger is one of the most destructive emotions when it's negative. Apply it to the negative state of anger. Remember that sometimes anger can be a positive force - when you or a loved one is being attacked for instance, anger can give you the strength you may need to escape danger. This is very rare so be brutally honest about any anger you may feel.

Anger has usually got some kind of fear at its base, so have a think about what you may be afraid of. If you get angry when someone insults you for instance, you may be afraid that others see you in the same way. Even if you think this is hogwash, give it a try, what can it hurt?

# Take the opportunity today to let go of any guilt you feel.

Guilt can be a debilitating emotion. This is closely linked to forgiveness - you must forgive yourself if you are to let go of guilt. Making amends is a good place to start if you're able. It might take a whole lot of courage so dig deep. Forgiveness really is the key to living a fulfilled life. Without it, you harbor negative thoughts to others and worse of all - to yourself.

> **66 Guilt: punishing yourself before God doesn't. 99**
>
> - Alan Cohen

NOVEMBER 6th

# Take the opportunity today to let go of any shame you feel.

Shame is a very personal emotion. Another which is closely linked to forgiveness and guilt. If you are ashamed of your behaviour in the past ask for forgiveness - say sorry. If your shame lies in who you are or how you look or how you feel - explore those thoughts. You are perfect. Your thoughts might not be, so investigate the root cause of those thoughts. If they are valid then forgive yourself. If they're not valid - let them go. If the way you feel shames you, go through the same process of whether those feelings are valid or invalid.

This is hard work I know, but the benefits are well worth it.

That's the last of the letting go guides - promise!

:)

NOVEMBER 8th

# Take the opportunity today to strike up a conversation with a stranger.

Before your friends were your friends they were strangers. We convert strangers into friends by communicating with them and finding out if they are on the same wavelength as us. But we meet strangers every day, when we go shopping or to the pub or to the gym or at the coffee shop or bus stop etc. Why do we decide to *not* convert them into friends? Probably because we don't have time for *more* friends - it's hard enough to see the ones we've got already, right? Maybe we feel a bit socially awkward about striking up conversations with strangers ad hoc.

You know what though, we don't have to try and convert everyone we meet into a new friend. We can just pass the time of day, interact, converse, be approachable, friendly - <u>nice!</u>

Wouldn't this make the day more pleasurable?

It goes without saying that you only do this in a safe environment - I remind you once more what the sergeant used to say on roll call each day in Hill Street Blues: '*Let's be careful out there!*'

> I try to make a point of communicating with everyone I meet starting with just a friendly 'Hi' or 'Alright'. Mostly people will respond in kind. A quick bit of friendly banter often follows and both of our days have been made brighter. :)

NOVEMBER 9th
# Take the opportunity today to stop waiting for everything to be perfect.

Are you one of those people that likes to think of themselves as a perfectionist? If you are, has anything you've ever done *been* perfect? I'm going to stick my neck out and guess not. The trouble with perfection is it's unattainable.

But...

It can be a great excuse for not finishing stuff.

Here's a suggestion...finish it. Whatever IT is, get it done, stop worrying about the possibility that there might be some errors in it or that some vital component might get omitted. Get it done then get it out there.

You can tinker with it and update it later, you'll get plenty of feedback I promise you. Stop worrying that it won't be perfect.

Now what excuse can you use for not finishing it?

---

Believe me I've been guilty of this myself in the past, and I'm sure I will again in the future. But here's the thing, I've noticed that the closer I get to finishing the more I want to spend time getting it 'just right'. I've learnt to be aware of those thoughts and filter them where necessary. (As I go through editing this book, I find myself drifting into that state again, I guarantee, the day I print this book I'll find things I want to correct or change. Too bad, moving on.)

NOVEMBER 10th

# Take the opportunity today to start a gratitude mantra.

A gratitude mindset is fundamental to achieving success, ask any highly successful person and they will tell you they were grateful <u>BEFORE</u> they were successful.

I have my mantra in my head and every now and then I add something new. I suggest you start off with 5 things you're grateful for in your life right now and add to them as and when you are able.

Either write them down in a pad with the title of that page something like:

'Things I'm grateful for in my life.' ...OR - memorise them.

Add to them as you realise something else you're really grateful for. Read this list or repeat in your mind every day (I do mine when I'm walking the dog).

Importantly - '*feel*' grateful as you go through the list.

Note: As you get used to this process add things that you might not have yet - eg: 'Thank you for the dream house I now live in.'

This '*acting as if*' is a powerful strategy as the mind doesn't actually discern between what's real and what's not - it only believes what you tell it.

Say 'Oh god, my life is so crap' or 'I'll never be able to earn that kind of money' or 'I'm no good at that' - and guess what? all those things will remain true!

Start thinking of things you want to be grateful for and act as if you already have them by including them in your gratitude mantra.

If this feels dumb - do it anyway, only you will know about it.

# Take the opportunity today to find reasons to agree.

Every day we find things to disagree with - well I do anyway! Whether it's items on the News or people I come into contact with, there's always some point of view that I either disagree with or find myself playing Devil's Advocate to. (People who know me are nodding their heads reading this!)

It's good to have a debate, it's how progress is often made. But often we support our point of view even when it becomes obvious we may be wrong - and that's why. We *hate* being wrong!

If however we go out of our way to agree from time to time we might find we change our standpoint about something which may in turn encourage someone else to change theirs. Apart from that, it's just nice to be in agreement on some things.

NOVEMBER 12th

# Take the opportunity today to be aware of any tension in your forehead, jaw or shoulders.

This might sound obvious, but how often during the day do you actually notice if you're tense? Take the opportunity today! Stop every hour or so and just sit for a moment and notice if you have any tension in your forehead, jaw or shoulders. These are the most common places to feel stress. If you notice tension - breathe deep and consciously relax that area of your body. Say to yourself: 'I notice when I'm tense and I relax.' Get your subconscious on board to help you.

This simple act could change your life, if you suffer from chronic back or neck pain this could really help. Imagine if you felt relaxed and free of pain all the time, wouldn't that make a difference?

# Take the opportunity today to thank everybody from your past because of where you are today and where you will be tomorrow.

You do realise that everything that has ever happened to you, good or bad, has brought you to where you are today. You may be in a great place right now, so think if any tiny little thing in your past were different it would have changed your trajectory and you may well be in a very different place right now rather than where you are. All those not so good places were necessary in order for you to be here.

If you're not in such a great place just realise that you are in one of those *not so good places* that will lead you to the great place later. So appreciate it for what it is. Why only appreciate it later? Thank everything and everybody from your past for helping to get you here. Thank 'here' for being part of the journey that's going to get you 'there' in the future.

I often thank one of my old bosses from my past employment for being such a difficult person to work for. It was his obnoxious ways that led me to quit and start my own business. :)

NOVEMBER 14th

# Take the opportunity today to do The Work.

*"The Work is a simple yet powerful process of inquiry that teaches you to identify and question the thoughts that cause all the suffering in the world. It's a way to understand what's hurting you, and to address the cause of your problems with clarity."*

That's how The Work by Byron Katie is described on her website. It's a process of identifying something that's troubling you then asking four questions about it:

1. Is what you're thinking <u>true</u>?
2. Can you <u>absolutely know</u> that it's true?
3. How do you react, what happens, when you believe that thought?
4. Who would you be <u>without</u> that thought?

After answering these four key questions you turn them around. Each turn around is an opportunity to experience the opposite of what you originally believed.

My advice is for you to go to the website and investigate this further if you have any negative thoughts about any issue that holds you back in life. Maybe from your childhood, maybe hurt you feel someone has inflicted on you, maybe your own limiting thoughts about yourself.

Go to: **www.thework.com/dothework.php** then click on 'Instructions for Doing The Work' on the right hand side

---

NOVEMBER 15th

# Take the opportunity today to be present and engaged.

What I mean by that is refrain from running on auto pilot. We all get into the flow of the day, doing this task and that. Having a coffee, then getting back to the grindstone. Walking the dog, having a bite for lunch, then back again to work. And we do it semi automatically, each day pretty much like the last.

Today, be more aware of your actions. Be more involved, consciously, in what you're doing. Savour each moment, enjoy it, live it, be grateful for it.

Of course there's a hundred and one things to do - you have to do them, just do them with awareness. Notice if time slows down or speeds up for you when you're more aware. It tends to slow down for me, which means I end up getting more done. Don't ask me how! Also I notice that because I'm paying more attention, what I do do gets done better. Walking the dogs for example, when it's a chore, my mind is roaming here and there and the dogs blend into the background. When I put all of my attention on them however, the whole experience is transformed. It's more fun, more rewarding.

Give it a go.

# Take the opportunity today to really look to see if you're recycling everything you possibly can.

Duh! Boring!

Yep, hear you, but... it needs to be done. We all have to do our bit. Natural resources are dwindling and so is the energy required to keep making stuff. Recycling is a way for the individual to play their part in responding to these issues. At home we now recycle about four times as much as we throw away - and we feel bad about *that*!

As we recycle more the process of recycling will become more efficient, which will make it more lucrative, which will result in more money being invested into making it more efficient and so on...

In the beginning a lot of recycling went straight to landfill just like normal rubbish, that's because it had to reach a certain level before business would get involved. I'm not saying that on occasion that doesn't still happen, but that shouldn't stop us doing our bit.

Take a look today - it's a rewarding feeling knowing you are doing all you can to minimise your footprint on this planet.

:)

NOVEMBER 17th

# Take the opportunity today to play a game.

My other half doesn't like to play games. She was an only child. I don't know why that should make a difference but that's what she says when I ask her why she doesn't.

I was one of five children so we were always playing games. Christmas time was a real game playing time of year for us as we'd all gather around the table to play Monopoly or Trivial Pursuit. I have fond memories of charades too which was always great fun, even for our parents - who were probably slightly tipsy at the time!

As I grew up I gravitated to Chess, Othello, Backgammon - one on one games where I could pit my wits against an individual opponent. I always found this to be excellent mental exercise as well as fun and a great way of momentarily ridding myself of life's stresses.

Maybe you already like to play games, if so, try a new game today.

The only opportunity I get to play these days is Chess against my computer. I only discovered the other day how to change the settings as in three years I'd never beaten it. I thought it must be stuck on Grandmaster level - sadly it was only halfway up the 'difficulty scale'. More practice needed I guess! :)

# Take the opportunity today to shop in a local store.

I'm sure that it's not only in the UK where our high streets are being stripped of independent shops and boutiques. Everywhere in the western world huge conglomerate companies are mopping up the consumer pound, dollar and euro by creating megastores where you can buy anything and everything. Whilst this is very convenient, the knock on effect is that local shops can't compete and go out of business. This leads to a homogenisation of the shopping experience. Everywhere is the same. The same big names selling the same big brands. The choice is diminishing rather than increasing. Also, entrepreneurs find it harder and harder to enter the market profitably.

Do yourself and your community a favour - especially at this time of year as we run up to the Christmas season, and shop locally at those independent stores that are still in business. Maybe that way they'll still be around in the New Year!

# Take the opportunity today to visit an awe inspiring building.

Whenever I go on holiday, anywhere, I'm always looking for interesting buildings to admire. I find it hard to walk past a beautiful church without going inside for a look around. There's a reason why religions put so much time, money and effort into creating fantastic architecture - it inspires us! It never ceases to amaze me that hundreds of years ago builders were able not only to design such incredible structures but were also able to build them. No cranes, no theodolites, no hightech machinery. Just craftsmanship and engineering prowess.

If you want to feel inspired there is no quicker way in my book than to experience something awesome in nature - and remember, *we* are in nature every bit as much as the great redwoods or termite mounds. Be inspired by what your fellow man has created and realise that you have the seed for that genius inside you, just waiting to manifest in your special way.

# Take the opportunity today to NOT watch TV. At All!

Need I say anymore?

Really?

OK, one thing. When we watch TV we don't need to use our imagination. The visual cortex is stimulated, as is the auditory sense. These are the two major senses needed to stimulate imagination. When we read for example we are imagining the scenes, imagining the voices and other sounds being described. With TV, that's all done for us.

So what?

Well, it makes us more suggestible! Why do you think so much money is spent on TV advertising? If that wasn't enough reason then why not allow yourself to 'think' for today. Just you and your thoughts. Hmm, maybe that's what some of us are trying to avoid.

If that is what you're trying to do, give yourself the benefit of the doubt today that through thinking you may just be able to see a route out of what you're trying to avoid.

Good luck with that.

# Take the opportunity today to imagine that everyone else are just aspects of yourself.

Imagine that everyone you see today, everyone you come in to contact with - is <u>You</u>.

If you meet someone annoying, imagine they are reflecting annoying aspects of You.

If you meet someone angry, imagine they are reflecting ways in which you become angry - do you remember being angry? What if someone saw you that day. What would they think about you? What are you thinking about that angry person you can see on the street, in the office, at the shops?

We are so quick to judge yet we hate being judged. This is a great exercise to apply to become less judgmental of others. When you think of them as being parts of You, you'll find it easier to ask yourself why they are behaving that way. Recognising that we have the potential to behave in the same way given the right circumstances allows us to empathise rather than criticise.

Try it.

NOVEMBER 22nd

# Take the opportunity today to contemplate your Be-Do-Have paradigm.

The brilliant Neale Donald Walsch writes:

*"The 'Be-Do-Have Paradigm' is one way of looking at life. This outlook on life, if reversed, could <u>change your life</u> - for the better. Because what is true about this paradigm is that most people have it all backwards."*

*"Most people started out (I know I did) with the understanding that how life worked was like this: Have-Do-Be. That is, when I HAVE the right stuff, I can DO the right things, and then I will get to BE what I want to be.*

*Example: When I HAVE enough money I can DO the thing called buy a house and I can BE the thing called secure. Want one more? Here goes: when I HAVE enough time I can DO the thing called take a vacation and I can BE the thing called rested and relaxed.*

*See how it works? This is how my father, my school, my society told me that it works. Life works this way. The only problem was, I was NOT getting to BE the things I thought I was going to get to BE after I had done all that I thought I had to DO, and had all the things that I thought I needed to HAVE. Or, if I did get to BE that, I only got to be it for a short period of time."*

I have paraphrased the above due to the room I have, but essentially life works: BE-DO-HAVE not HAVE-DO-BE. Look at your life to date this way, and see what you recognise.

To find out about N. D. Walsch visit: **www.NealeDonaldWalsch.com**

NOVEMBER 23rd
# Take the opportunity today to play Devil's Advocate.

Anyone that knows me knows this is my favourite standpoint.

Not because I want to be obstinate. It's because I think the most interesting debates happen when not everyone is in agreement. I take the Devil's Advocate standpoint when I do agree - just to open the discussion to alternate ideas. From this standpoint it's only a small step to consider changing your belief about something too.

This can become quite heated so put your diplomacy hat on.

> " Debate and convergence of views can only enrich our history and culture. "
>
> - Ibrahim Babangida

NOVEMBER 24th
# Take the opportunity today to investigate.

You can apply this to anything you want. Investigate how something works if you want. Investigate why some things happens the way they do, or why some belief systems believe the things they do. Investigate some historical fact or how the chain of events in nature lead to certain outcomes. Investigate investment opportunities or business opportunities. Investigate why you think the way you do about certain things or why you do the things you do.

Basically, just kick start your investigative side today - who knows what you'll find.

:)

NOVEMBER 25th

# Take the opportunity today to ask: 'What would I want to happen by the end of today?'

A YouTube video inspired me to include this question in the book. A film crew asked dozens of people randomly on the street this single question. The answers were mesmerising and comical, inspiring and engaging. It set me on a path to create my own viral video asking a different question. Maybe that's how you found this book in the first place.

Anyway, ask yourself this question, dwell on it for a moment, then see what comes to mind.

# Take the opportunity today to imagine you could talk with anyone from history. What would you ask them?

Can you imagine how brilliant that would be? Anyone at all. Ask them anything. What would you ask? More importantly, how would they answer? That is the point of this exercise. Allow your subconscious to decide how you think that incredible person from history would answer your question.

Get a pad, write your question down, then sit for a while imagining in as much detail as possible that person from history answering. Write their answer under your question. Write it as quickly as possible - ask them to slow down for you if you need to, they will. But capture their answer as quickly as it comes so that your own mind doesn't try and filter or censor it.

This is a great way to tap into your own wisdom and intuition.

NOVEMBER 27th

# Take the opportunity today to understand what your pain might mean.

Certain therapies will associate specific pains with particular mental issues. They say it's our mind's way of showing us the solution to a problem we might be experiencing. The mind manifests a physical representation of the issue in an attempt to get you to *look* at it.

For instance, knee pain can be due to your sense of direction in life as the knees are integral to you physically changing direction. Shoulder pain may signify you are trying to reach for something you deem '*out of reach*'. Debilitating back pain could be the mind telling you that you need to rest your body completely. (Obvious really!)

The next time you experience pain that hasn't been caused externally by a fall for example, ask yourself what that area of your body might signify. What might your mind be trying to tell you.

Of course all pain could be a response to the body suffering physical damage so get it checked out if you're worried.

All during this year I have been suffering from 'frozen shoulder' - a term used to describe a pain that has no obvious physical cause. When my instructor asked me what I thought was out of my reach I realised this very book seemed to be, at the time. By addressing my doubts about whether I could actually complete it I have managed to heal what three physios couldn't do in 12 months! I still sought help from a fourth in case there was a physical cause but I'm convinced that when my mind was in the right place my body allowed itself to be healed.

# Take the opportunity today to do something differently.

If you're a creature of habit like me then doing things differently goes against the grain. I actually advocate in the strongest terms that making certain tasks habitual is integral to you getting them done. Having said that, by doing things a bit differently from time to time we step out of the boredom of routine, we engage our minds and our creativity and we give ourselves the opportunity to find a new way. A better way maybe.

By doing this often we may find that the way we *are* doing something is the best way - so we get reassurance. But we may find new interesting, time saving, stress relieving ways that would otherwise remain unknown. Engage someone else in this process and your combined efforts may reap rich rewards.

You'll only know by trying.

# Take the opportunity today to challenge the status quo.

No, I don't mean write a letter to the band asking them why they only use three chords!

I'm talking about *your* status quo. Is your life just ticking along? Are you moving towards your goals or just treading water? Are you doing all you can to get the life you want or residing in your comfort zone? Are you making excuses for why your life is the way it is?

Examine this, give it some real thought, ask the difficult questions. If you can't do it yourself at first, ask a trusted friend or family member to ask.

Somebody once said *'If you're not growing, you're dying'* and as morbid as it sounds it's right.

NOVEMBER 30th

# Take the opportunity today to review the guides of this month to see which ones you may have missed.

Did you expect to get this far? I sincerely hope you have noticed some changes in your life since starting to read this book and implement it's guides. Keep going over this month's guides as often as you can to give yourself the best chance of noticing one that will grab your attention. I've said it at the end of every month and I'll say it again, it's those guides that grab you that you should put most effort into doing. From the hundreds in this book I'm 100% certain many will prove useful, inspirational, motivational and ultimately life changing.

---

Make a note in your journal or diary of any changes you have noticed since you started this book.

---

DECEMBER 1st

# Take the opportunity today to learn the Listen-Act-Trust Process.

I learnt this technique from Lisa Sasevich (the Queen of sales conversion and developer of the Invisible Close) whilst she was being interviewed by John Assaraf. It stands for:

**L**isten - to your intuition

**A**ct - on what you feel, and

**T**rust - yourself and the action you are taking in response

This is great advice. All to often we allow our minds to get in the way and cast seeds of doubt over our plans. Apply this process daily to each and every circumstance that arises.

To find out more about Lisa Sasevich go to:

**www.LisaSasevich.com**

# Take the opportunity today to consider what is stopping you getting what you want.

Do you ever wonder what is stopping you? Do you *think* it's outside influences? Do you think that other people's decisions affect your life more than your decisions? Think again. You are holding on to the steering wheel of your life, of course if you see a pothole steer around it. If you hit a pothole and bust a tyre, stop, get it fixed, then continue.

Your decisions are what make your life, they dictate your circumstances way more than any other outside occurrences. Now take some time and figure out what is stopping you make the decisions that will take you towards the life you desire.

DECEMBER 3rd

# Take the opportunity today to do one thing at a time.

After a dinner party you look at the clearing up and think: '*God where do I start?*' But you start. You start somewhere, anywhere and you keep going until a couple of hours later everything is clear and tidy again.

Overwhelm is a huge influencer of inertia. Not knowing where to start can hinder us from starting at all. It's tempting to think that all the great people of history that ever achieved anything had it all figured out. Well they didn't! Most of them anyhow, were just like you and me except they got past their overwhelm. They just started and then figured out the next step, then the next. Sometimes it became apparent they took the wrong step so they went back and started again. That's not a waste of time. Not starting, procrastinating - that's a waste of time.

So get going, start, get moving. Once the train is in motion it takes less and less energy to keep it in motion.

DECEMBER 4th

# Take the opportunity today to dedicate the day to doing what one of your loved ones wants.

Could be your spouse, one of your kids, your parent, a friend, even your dog! Dedicate this day to them. Find out what they'd like to do and help them in achieving that. Make it your goal today to do what they want. When it's *your* goal, you'll feel no resentment for what you might be missing. When it's *your* goal, you'll be motivated rather than obligated.

If you manage to achieve the goal of helping your loved one do what they want you'll feel good about it. They might even decide that tomorrow it's your turn, so get thinking about what you want.

:)

I want breakfast in bed, followed by a nice shoulder rub, then maybe an hour to myself with cup of tea and a good book. Then I'd like a nice lunch please, maybe at the pub, followed by an hour on the sofa watching something funny. In the evening I'd like to go to a nice restaurant and maybe take in a show. Just in case you were wondering. :)

DECEMBER 5th

# Take the opportunity today to connect your problems and desires.

Often the solution to a problem can be found in the *desire* associated with solving it. EG: My other half Em suffers from Non-completion Syndrome, the tasks she does at work never seem to end. She knows full well that if they did they'd be followed by more things to do but that's ok. Imagine having a To Do list that never got ticked off. It just kept growing and growing. The tasks on it moved forwards here and there but they never finished.

A milkman for example has the same task each day. Seemingly never ending, except that each and every day he completes the task of delivering the milk. Next day he starts again, and completes it again. Tick. Done. Next. A sense of closure, of achievement.

If you have a similar situation at work or at home or in any other area of your life where things never seem to get finished try this: break the task down into smaller parts. Create achievable tasks so that you can tick them off as done. The bigger picture may continue unended but at least it's constituent parts can, piece by piece, get finished. Make the tasks as small as you want, but separate them from the whole. This will go some way to relieving the stress believe me.

# Take the opportunity today to find a word in the dictionary you don't know and learn what it means.

To a lot of you that might sound a bit dull, but I love learning stuff. This is just about the easiest and quickest way to learn something new. Plus, you immediately increase your vocabulary. Then you have to find a way of dropping that new word into conversation casually! :)

Whilst looking, you may well surprise yourself with how many words you do know. *And* you'll get better at Scrabble!

**Mousseline** /'moohsline/ *n* **1** a fine sheer fabric (eg: of rayon) that resembles muslin. **2** a frothy sauce, eg: a hollandaise sauce that has whipped cream or eggs added to it.

## DECEMBER 7th

# Take the opportunity today to write a script of your next 12 months, make it spectacular and detailed.

This is a bit like your perfect day except it could be your perfect year! Just like your perfect day exercise, make it fantastic, exciting and inspirational. Allow everything you would love to happen, happen. As you write it down and let it pour out you will actually start coming up with strategies and tactics that will help you get what you want. So, this isn't just wishful thinking, this is actually a bone fide way of accessing your subconscious mind in order to help you figure out how to move forward in all sorts of ways.

Remember, if you don't try any of these exercise you'll never know if they work for you, so go get a pen and a pad and a cup of coffee and spend a little time describing your next 12 months.

# Take the opportunity today to do something out of character.

This may prove to be more difficult than you first imagine. We are programmed to behave in a certain way plus we have definite character traits - a combination of nature and nurture. To operate outside of your own personality will seem alien but give it a go.

By doing this you will discover alternate behaviours, some which you may like and some which you won't. The ones you like you can adopt and the ones you don't will solidify your existing traits.

EG: If you normally give money to people in the street and today you decide not to, you may feel really guilty or selfish or judgmental. Those feelings will enforce your usual behaviour of giving. Alternatively, if you normally keep your head down at work and don't converse much with your colleagues, today may prove to be a real eye opener. If you make a concerted effort to talk with or help a colleague you may find a friend or they may return the help on another day. This may set you off helping more and more colleagues in the future.

Give this some thought today as I fully understand that this might not be easy to get your head around at first. Once you do, it could change your life!

DECEMBER 9th

# Take the opportunity today to be a copycat.

I used to have ideas about business opportunities all the time. I used to get really excited about the potential success within the concept. Sadly, they all came to nothing. Until, I realised why.

It wasn't that the ideas were not valid, it was I had no idea *how* to make them happen. After my revelation (see my case study p.76) I realised that I didn't need to figure out the *how*. Somebody else must have done something similar in the past, so I just needed to find who, then how *they* did it. That way I could just copy *their* process. This is often referred to as 'modelling'. I have since modelled other people's successes in many areas and I hope I'll continue to do so in many others.

So, if you have a goal and you're finding it difficult to figure out how to achieve it, try copying how someone else achieved something similar.

The phrase *'Why try and reinvent the wheel'* springs to mind.

DECEMBER 10th

# Take the opportunity today to write down a lesson you've learned.

By analysing a lesson you have learned in the past you will automatically discover how you did it. Writing what you learned is a powerful first step. By writing it you get it out of your head and into some sort of order on the page. From there it can be re-ordered, re-read and re-*alised*.

It will become apparent what the process was and you'll be able to apply that knowledge to other lessons you may need to learn.

This is a good way to structure it;

1. Explain what your situation was before you learnt the lesson

2. Describe what happened that allowed you to learn

3. Explain what's different now due to the learning

This will give you a start point to get the memories around it clear.

This is the structure I used to help my Case Study volunteers communicate their story. It helps to chop some information up into chunks so that they are more manageable. The chunks can be rearranged afterwards if necessary.

## DECEMBER 11th
# Take the opportunity today to practice your vision.

By that I mean rather than seeing what *is*, see what *can be*.

Many of the guides in this book are similar to each other, that's not because I couldn't think of enough, on the contrary, I have enough to fill two books. The point is that sometimes we need to look at the same thing from different angles sometimes. To get a different perspective.

So, I urge you again today to imagine what your life could be like. Visualise what you want it to be like. Meditate on the way you want to live. Daydream about how you will live each day. These tactics get easier the more you do them, so practice. Meditate one day, daydream the next. Visualise on another day and imagine the next. As I've mentioned many times in this book already, when you do this you allow your subconscious mind to start *showing* you the way.

We are all wise beyond our conscious thoughts, we just need to allow ourselves to be. And that takes practice.

DECEMBER 12th

# Take the opportunity today to consider all of your strengths.

This might sound like a waste of time at first, I mean, you know your strengths don't you? Don't you?

Well maybe you do or maybe you don't, but try this little exercise to help you discern how your strengths in one area of your life could help in another.

Write down these six areas of your life:
Health, Family, Relationships, Work, Personal Growth, and Fun.
Now write down your strengths in each, for instance under Health you might put; I eat healthily, exercise regularly, maintain my ideal weight. Under Work you might put; I always hit my targets, I spot new opportunities, I create efficient systems and processes etc.

Once you have completed all six lists in as much detail as possible, compare your strengths in one area to the other areas of your life. You may find that strengths in one area could transfer to another except you've never thought to. Because we compartmentalise our lives we sometimes can't see how our behaviour in one area could help another. Maybe you're methodical and efficient at work but hopelessly disorganised on a social level or at home. Consider what enables your strength in a particular area and apply that process in another part of your life if it will improve it.

On the flip side, you may like your personal life to be spontaneous and chaotic!

# Take the opportunity today to dream a solution.

I've mentioned many times throughout this book the value of getting in touch with your subconscious, well this guide is about getting in touch with your unconscious.

Huh?

We all dream at night - whether we remember or not. It's part of the brain's process for gaining proper rest from the conscious waking hours. Through studies on sleep deprivation and other techniques it's becoming more apparent that our unconscious is actually processing information whilst resting. We are able to actually tap into that processing if we just put the right programming in at the right time.

Tonight, just before you go to sleep, consider a problem or issue you are experiencing. Something that has you stumped. Then ask yourself to dream the solution. Start the request: '*How can I...*' then fill in the blank. Repeat it a few times over and over.

EG: 'How can I find a better job doing [xyz]?' or,
'How can I get motivated to [xyz]?' or,
'How can I find the right partner for me?' etc.

You get the idea. Your mind will actually process this last command of the day and you may well dream the solution. Or the solution may come to you throughout the next day. Have a go and see what happens, I have certainly had some success applying this.

# Take the opportunity today to be a thermostat and <u>not</u> a thermometer.

One sets the environment the other reads it. I learned this from Mary Morrisey.

What do I mean by that? Well, if you find yourself reacting to the hassles of everyday life, never knowing what'll show up, then you are being a thermometer. It's all happening '*out there*' and you react accordingly. Of course there's an awful lot happening '*out there*', for ALL of us. However, if you are *making* the decisions, being *proactive* instead of *reactive* you are *creating* the circumstances of your life. You're setting your environment like a thermostat.

I know, I know, not all the time, not in every circumstance - even a hermit living in a cave is subject to the weather. But the more you set your own circumstances, the more you take responsibility for what is happening to you and *how* you react *to* it, the more control you will feel. That's what we want after all, isn't it? To feel in control of our own lives.

Consider today whether you are acting as much like a thermostat as you could. If not, take charge of how things make you feel. Decide *how* you want to feel. I'll be giving you some tips on how you can do that very shortly.

## DECEMBER 15th
# Take the opportunity today to practice "The Process".

Dave Austin is a 'mental performance coach' that has helped many of the world's top athletes achieve extraordinary results. This is his 5 step system which he calls "The Process"- a method that gets his clients '*in the zone*' and helps them to stay there longer.

**1** - Appreciate nature close up, focus on three things in nature to appreciate; the bark of a tree, a blade of grass etc.

**2** - Imagine yourself surrounded with white energy, see it as extremely positive and loving. Then imagine your family and friends surrounded with that white energy. Lastly imagine someone you don't like or who you've had an argument with and surrounded them with white energy as well.

**3** - Focus on what you're grateful for and get into the powerful energy of gratitude.

**4** - Visualize - walk through an imagined gate whilst thinking about all the things you're grateful for - step into the beauty of nature that surrounds you in this place. Allow the feeling of amazement. Breathe in the positive and breathe out the negative.

**5** - Creative Expression - step through another gate, one that leads to your ideal life. See yourself living that life, enjoying it fully. Once you are finished, walk back through both of your gates, open your eyes, then write your thoughts down - uncensored. Whatever comes, write it down.

Your mind will probably wander quite a bit the first few times you try this, but that's ok. Keep practicing and enjoy what comes out of this experience. If you've gotten this far through the book, then none of the above will surprise you. As these are things that the world's top coaches use effectively in business, sports and the areas of self-improvement and use in their day to day interactions with the best of the best in the world.

To see a great video of Dave explaining "The Process" in more detail visit: **www.ExtremeMentalFocus.com**

For more info on Dave also visit: **www.ExceedPotential.com**

DECEMBER 16th

# Take the opportunity today to over-deliver.

I have lived by this motto all my working life. (Which started about age 10 as a milk boy.) Over-delivering is going the extra mile, giving 110%, delivering more than you're paid to. This sounds alien to a lot of people especially the over 50's that I know. A lot of them have a Union mindset. When I say, that I don't mean to be derogatory - I absolutely believe in Unions and the protection they give to company employees. The mentality I'm talking about is doing *more* than you're paid to. By doing *more* the Union's might argue you're denying someone else from having that job. That may be true if enough employees were over-delivering but the logical extension of that argument is for everybody to work less, that way many more people would have jobs. It doesn't make sense to me. If you want to succeed in life you have to learn to over-deliver, surprise people, whether they're your employer or your customer. When you over-deliver you raise your head above the crowd, you get noticed. You may make enemies along the way - but that is their problem. Who wants to be mediocre, just doing what they need to and no more? Not me. You?

If you want to succeed in any area of your life; work, relationships, personal ambitions etc. deliver as much value as you possibly can.

# Take the opportunity today to realise the universe is a 'feeling' mirror.

When I say that I mean it reflects back what you put out.

If you put out fear, fear is reflected back on you. If you put out worry, worry is reflected back on you. If you put out love, kindness, understanding, compassion, trust, loyalty - guess what? They are the things reflected back on you.

So take a minute and ask yourself what you *feel* most days. Then ask yourself, honestly, if that is what you are putting out in the world. If you think this is rubbish put it to the test. If you feel fear or worry or lack or hate or used or untrustful or resentful, consider reversing those feelings just for a day. Trust people, no matter what. Be kind to people, no matter what. Forgive everyone of everything, no matter what. Imagine that everything you worry about is going to turn out just fine, no matter what. Decide not to be afraid of anything, no matter what. <u>Just for today</u>.

Do this as authentically as you possibly can, it'll be hard, but do it. Then see how you feel tomorrow. If you noticed a difference, however small, do it again, and again. Before you know it you may be feeling all of those positive feelings mentioned above because that is what you'll then be putting out.

DECEMBER 18th

# Take the opportunity today to be your best.

I remember many years ago listening to Muhammad Ali in an interview. The interviewer asked: '*What would you have been if you were not a boxer?*' Ali replied: '*The Best!*' He went on to explain that if he had been a road sweeper, he would have been the best road sweeper. No matter what he would have done, he would have been the best at it. What an incredible attitude.

This exemplifies the attitude of success. That being the best in whatever you are doing is the way to move forward. That doesn't mean you have to *become* the best, after all, only one person can be the best. The important thing is to strive to be the best. It's this striving that ensures you deliver to others and to yourself. We all feel good about ourselves when we've done a great job - even if it's only fixing a shelf at home or helping to build a shed at the local scout club. The boost to our self esteem is a great motivator.

So, strive to be the best at whatever you do, even if you don't want to be doing it. At least that way *you'll* get more out of the task and you may just get noticed by the next person to help you along the path to success.

> **66 It isn't the mountains ahead to climb that wear you out; it's the pebble in your shoe. 99** - Muhammad Ali

## DECEMBER 19th

# Take the opportunity today to ignore negative comments and naysayers.

Unless others have DONE what you want to do they are not speaking from experience when they offer their advice. When they say "*I think...*" followed by a negative comment - ignore it. Thank them, because I'm sure they mean well and don't want you to fail or get hurt - but ignore their advice.

When someone starts a sentence "*I think...*" it's usually because they don't '<u>know</u>'. And if they don't know why would you listen? It goes without saying then that those that start a sentence "*I don't think...*" have already nailed their colours to the mast, ie: They *don't* think. You know the ones, they say things like: "*I don't think that would work*" or "*I don't think you should do it that way*" or "*I don't think people think that way.*" Unless they have a lot of evidence to back up what they DON'T think - ignore them too. Again - kindly and with thanks.

The only way to get what you want is to take action and lots of it. Failure is testing in disguise. As long as you learn from it, it will be your greatest teacher. The world is full of people who don't live the lives they want because they don't take enough action because they think they'll be wasting their time trying stuff before they've figured out every last detail. They're called 'procrastinators' - I know, I used to be one.

So, move forward with your plans, take the actions you feel you should, be prepared to make mistakes and even to fail, but, please don't allow someone else with less get-up-and-go than you, to dissuade you from your course. You'll regret it - not them!

## DECEMBER 20th
# Take the opportunity today to consider your death.

I know that seems a bit morbid but stick with me a moment.

*"Remembering that I'll be dead soon is the most important tool I've ever encountered to help me make the big choices in life. Because almost everything - all external expectations, all pride, all fear of embarrassment or failure - these things just fall away in the face of death, leaving only what is truly important. Remembering that you are going to die is the best way I know to avoid the trap of thinking you have something to lose. You are already naked. There is no reason not to follow your heart. Stay hungry. Stay foolish."* - Steve Jobs on leaving Apple, Aug 2011

Steve Jobs was prompted into thoughts of death by medical problems, but WE don't have to be. From your brimming with health self - consider death and let it be your driving force to take action.

To quote Nike - *'Just Do It!'*

### DECEMBER 21st

## Take the opportunity today to learn something new.

Every time we learn something new we not only learn something about the wider world in which we live but also about ourselves. We, after all, are the filter to the world in which we live. When we learn something about it that we didn't know before we get a new perspective on things. We can formulate a different opinion or at least adapt our present one. This is growth and that after all is what we are here for.

> " Lord grant me the serenity to accept the things I can not change, courage to change the things I can. And the wisdom to know the difference. "

- Reinhold Niebuhr

DECEMBER 22nd

# Take the opportunity today to use Napoleon Hill's technique of Independent Council.

Napoleon Hill wrote the ground breaking book: 'Think and Grow Rich' back in the 1930s. It has subsequently become one of the foremost books to read for any successful entrepreneur. Pretty much every millionaire businessman on the planet has read it and applied it's philosophy. Yet you don't need to be an entrepreneur to get immense value from it. I highly recommend it to anyone who wants to get more out of life in any area.

One of the techniques he advocates is seeking Independent Council. This is a mind technique of significant power. You must be able to turn off your '*this is silly*' button, and turn on your '*let's pretend*' button instead. This will enable you to use this technique to tap into your own subconscious wisdom.

So, find somewhere comfortable and quiet. Relax for a few minutes until you are calm and a bit daydreamy. Now imagine a big oak panelled door on the other side of the room or maybe a big oak tree if you are outside. Now imagine that anyone from history comes to join you through that door or from behind that tree. They sit with you, as many of them as you want. When they are all there, ask your question. Something you are struggling with. Ask their advice and listen carefully to what they say. The wisdom your subconscious associates with those individuals will allow you to find the answer which they will voice.

Listen!

DECEMBER 23rd
# Take the opportunity today to use your anger.

We all get angry from time to time and it's generally regarded as a personality flaw. Well it's NOT! It's only a flaw if you allow it to become destructive. The recent Arab Spring Uprising grew out of the anger felt by people in the middle east at being oppressed. One of the first protests started in Egypt with citizens gathering on the streets wearing black and simply joining hands. Their anger brought them out but they were not destructive. Anger can be a calling to act.

So today, I urge you to use any anger you're feeling to manifest a change. Maybe a change in your home, your work environment, your community or your country. Get outraged, but make it constructive rather than destructive. Ensure something positive results from any action you take. Allow your anger to get you involved in making a positive difference.

DECEMBER 24th

# Take the opportunity today to consider all of your labels.

I don't mean the ones in the back of your shirt or blouse. I mean the ones that you and other people tag you with; mum, wife, volunteer, colleague, writer, coach - whatever they are. Write them all down, as many as you can think of. Ask, your spouse or your kids or your friends to help identify them for you if you need to.

Once you have that list give it a read through. Understand what each of those labels mean to you and to everyone that knows you. Realise how connected you are through those labels. Realise how important you are to all of those people.

Now realise that you are not *just* those labels. You are any label you want to be. Consider what other labels you would like to be defined by. Champion Skydiver maybe? Successful Business Owner? Mover and Shaker in the field of [xyz]? Guitar Legend? Explorer?

You get the idea - you are unlimited.

DECEMBER 25th

# Take the opportunity today to preview your future.

I know you were probably expecting a guide centred around connecting with your family, considering peace, love and understanding and all that. And that is something I hope you do anyway, I mean this is the day for that after all.

So, after you've enjoyed all the gift exchanging, gorged enough food to fill a small people carrier and are relaxing on the sofa, take a moment to consider your future. What will it look like? What do you want it to look like? Run your future through your mind like a movie trailer. You rarely go to the cinema before seeing a trailer of the film, right? You want to know you're going to enjoy it. Well, do that with your life! See it in as much detail as possible, make it big, make it colourful, make it loud.

Then, make it happen!


Happy Christmas!

:)

# Take the opportunity today to put your labels in priority order.

On Christmas Eve you had the opportunity to write a list of your labels - I hope you had the chance to do that. It's a busy time of year after all. If you managed it, today take a few minutes to put it in priority order. Find out what's most important to you. It may surprise you.

Ensure you have added the labels you aspire to before you do this part. If there are any other labels you still want to collect, list them first before prioritising. This will enable you to see what goals are really important to you still. Way back earlier in the year, I hope you did the Passion Test (July 30th) in order to get clear on this. Now you have another opportunity to see if you still feel the same.

## DECEMBER 27th
# Take the opportunity today to swallow the frog.

This is a piece of Advice from International Business Coach, Brian Tracy. He suggests you spend the first 30 minutes of every day doing the most uncomfortable thing. Get it out of the way or at least break the back of it. None of us wants to swallow a frog, right - not even the French!

By doing this uncomfortable task first you set yourself up to succeed for the rest of the day. That thing won't play on your mind all morning, then all afternoon as you think of excuse after excuse to avoid it. Days later it could still be sitting there, becoming even more uncomfortable. Get up and get it done then get on with the rest of your day. You'll feel better for it.

To find out more about the legend that is Brian Tracy go to:
**www.BrianTracy.com**

DECEMBER 28th

# Take the opportunity today to consider the choices you make.

Your entire life is the result of the choices you have made. And I don't necessarily mean your external life. If you've been run over by a bus sometime in your life - chances are it wasn't your fault. But how you reacted to it happening was your choice. Yes. It was.

So, where are you in your life? If you're not exactly where you want to be (most of us aren't) then consider *why* that is. Start with: Am I moving towards my goals, away from my goals or just standing still? The answer to that question will bring up another 'why?' If you're not moving towards your goals it may be down to your paradigms, your belief systems. Do you believe you're not capable? Don't deserve it? Aren't worthy? Aren't well enough connected? Don't have enough money? What?

None of those are real reasons. So dig a bit deeper. Whatever you find will be a choice you're making. Look at what you want and I would bet my house that someone somewhere has overcome the same hurdles as you to get it. Which means...you can too. You might have to find out what choices they made and copy them. You might just have to break the steps necessary to achieve your goal down into smaller chunks so you can have a better chance of achieving it.

Look at your choices today

# Take the opportunity today to consider whether your happiness is created by your conditions or the other way around.

'*Happiness is not created as a result of certain conditions, certain conditions are created as a result of happiness.*' Neale Donald Walsch said that and I agree with him. And this applies to all states of mind.

What he means is if you are a happy person then you will create happy conditions around you. A truly happy person doesn't need the external conditions to be a certain way in order to be happy. Easier said than done right. Of course it is, at first. What's the big secret then? Well, for me, it's just to accept what is. Strive for X but be happy with Y. Not getting attached to the outcome.

When I watch a football match I see the two sets of supporters cheering their team on and in the end one team wins and the other loses, usually. The losing supporters are often devastated. Why? Because they are attached to the outcome. They strive for X (their team winning) but they're not happy with Y (their team losing). They make *themselves* unhappy.

Take a look today at areas in your life where you might be doing this. And if you think that by adopting this mental state you'll lose out on the highs in life (like your team winning) think again. You can continue striving as much as you ever did - but now you won't be affected by the lows.

DECEMBER 30th

# Take the opportunity today to review all of your goals.

We've covered a lot of ground over the course of this book and remember, on January 1st you can start again. Make this a daily practice every year and the changes to your life will mount up to something incredible. Today, review all the goals you've had since starting to read this book - how many have you achieved? How many have you made significant steps toward? Pat yourself on the back for your achievements.

Now read your goals lists again. If some are done, then reprioritise what remain. Have you thought of more goals you want to add? Consider how you achieved the ones that are done. Is there a pattern? Is there a behaviour you adopt that helps you achieve them?

Reviewing in this way will allow you to become even clearer on how to move forward with the other goals on your list. New Year's Day is just 48 hours away, so get your list organised so you are ready to start again.

I wish you all the success for the coming year ahead.

DECEMBER 31st

# Take the opportunity today to ask yourself these three questions...

Do I Live? Do I Love? Do I Matter?

Brendon Burchard of Experts Academy fame and author of *Life's Golden Ticket* poses three similar questions to his audiences and readers. He uses the past tense 'Did I...' It stems from the near death experience he had a few years ago. He was in a car accident that should have killed him, and as the car rolled over, seemingly in slow motion, the three questions: Did I Live? Did I Love? Did I Matter? ran through his mind.

If *you* were faced with death, he proposes these same questions would run through your own mind.

I suggest you don't wait until it's that late. I suggest you ask the questions above at the end of each year. At the end of each month, each week and at the end of each day. If you can ask these three powerful questions at the end of each day you will start to live the next day with more purpose, more life and more love, day after day, after day.

To learn more about Brendon and the great wisdom he has to offer I encourage you to take a look at his website:

**www.BrendonBurchard.com**

you'll find many inspiring videos there amongst many other great resources.

---

# Summing up

Now you have reached the end of this book you have not reached the end of your journey. If like me you missed many many opportunities then simply start the whole process again tomorrow. Go back to the beginning of the book, revisit your lists that you made right at the start. Re-write them now and see what's changed. Then, start over. This book can be used again and again every year. There will always be new guides to challenge you even if you did them the first time around, doing them again may have a completely different effect on you or someone else.

Review the changes you wanted to see in your life and write down any changes that you have noticed.

I would love to hear of any stories of how this book may have helped you to make changes in your life. If you would like to share them please email your story to: **stuart.young40@googlemail.com** and with your permission I may just include it in my upcoming book: **"Life's Rich Harvest - Stories of Change"**. Simply start with where you were in your life, followed by what changed, ending with where you are now in your life.

If you would like to go through the life changing process I explained in my case study (p.76) and you have completed the FREE 90 Day Mindset Changing Program that came with this book (not available for Kindle purchases), then you might be interested in my 90 Day Advanced Mindset Mastery Program. Just go to:

**www.AdvancedMindsetMastery.com** to find more details.

# Acknowledgements

Typically an author works alone in creating whatever book they are working on, some are lucky enough to have an editor that helps with the direction etc. Over and above that there are usually many, many other people that help in the creation of a book, some without even realising it. In creating this book I would like to thank Em for being patient and understanding throughout, her input along the way has helped steer me in directions I wouldn't have thought of myself. Thanks to Hannah for being a constant inspiration in my life. Thanks to all of my friends - you know who you are.

To my parents who raised me with a questioning mind without which I would never have begun this journey. (Without realising it my mum started the ball rolling when she gave me José Silva's 'Silva Mind Control' book over 20 years ago.) To my Case Study volunteers, your stories are the glue that hold the chapters together, thank you Donna, Claire, Tina and Vicky. Thanks to everyone that gave me feedback on the cover design - I'm sorry if your choice was not the one I used!

Thanks to my program volunteers: Jo Kinnaird, Niki Torbett, Jo Joslyn, Samantha Rothwell, Hannah Young, Sandra Green, Sian Darvill, Claire Hipkin and especially Gareth Smith who started that whole ball rolling.

Thanks especially to all those huge names in the field of peak performance and self improvement that agreed to have their techniques and strategies featured in this book, including in no particular order: Hale Dwoskin, Brian Tracy, Dan Sullivan, John Assaraf, Scott Ginsberg, Lisa Sasevich, Dean Jackson, Noah St. John, Frank Kern, Burt Goldman and Dave Austin.

Thanks to all of my street video volunteers: Loredana Sciaraffa, Roger King, Joy Mills, Rachel Crowhurst, Kiran Paruchuri, Doreen Worcester, Andrew Shelbourn, Louis Smart, Laraine Edwards, James Howkins, Gavin Kane, Nathan Felix, Oshadie Karunatilake, Dave Pymble, Emily Dowling, Jake Plaskitt, Elizabeth McLaughlin, Chris Ford, Michelle Woolford, Jessica Rushforth, Mike Odongo, Brigitte Wright, Ellen White, Katrina Jones, Samantha Willis, Georgina Cattani, Antony Hodgson, Luke Mehmi, Carolyn McKinnon-Harrison. Thanks to Chris Ferris for his invaluable help and great attitude. And to Mick McEvoy for being a catalyst. :)

# INDEX

# How To Change Your Life One Day At A Time

Take the opportunity today to plant something. 315
Take the opportunity today to entertain some kids by being daft. 316
Take the opportunity today to accept. 317
Take the opportunity today to notice any aches or pains - then let them go. 318
Take the opportunity today to ask yourself a positive question. 319
Take the opportunity today to be daft for your own amusement! 320
Take the opportunity today to make yourself a cuppa and just sit and enjoy it. 321
Take the opportunity today to get in touch with your envy. 322
Take the opportunity today to understand your dissatisfaction. 323
Take the opportunity today to act as if. 324
Take the opportunity today to Scramble a bad memory. 325
Take the opportunity today to let go of any grudge you feel. 326
Take the opportunity today to get rid of something from your house you don't need. 327
Take the opportunity today to think about who you admire and why. 328
Take the opportunity today to notice when you're comparing yourself to others
- then STOP. 329
Take the opportunity today to write a list of things that you are afraid of. 330
Take the opportunity today to write the opposite of being afraid. 331
Take the opportunity today to ignore any negative comments you hear. 332
Take the opportunity today to chunk down. 333
Take the opportunity today to chunk up. 334
Take the opportunity today to accept your mistakes. 335
Take the opportunity today to accept your friend's mistakes. 336
Take the opportunity today to start a philosophers club. 337
Take the opportunity today to trust. 338
Take the opportunity today to be mindful - stare at something for 10 minutes. 340
Take the opportunity today to make something. 341
Take the opportunity today to review the guides of this month to see which ones you
may have missed. 342

## November

Take the opportunity today to practice letting go. 346
Take the opportunity today to let go of any hate you feel. 347
Take the opportunity today to let go of any feelings of inadequacy. 348
Take the opportunity today to let go of any jealousy you feel. 349
Take the opportunity today to let go of any anger you feel. 350
Take the opportunity today to let go of any guilt you feel. 351
Take the opportunity today to let go of any shame you feel. 352
Take the opportunity today to strike up a conversation with a stranger. 353
Take the opportunity today to stop waiting for everything to be perfect. 354
Take the opportunity today to start a gratitude mantra 355
Take the opportunity today to find reasons to agree. 356
Take the opportunity today to be aware of any tension in your forehead, jaw
or shoulders. 357
Take the opportunity today to thank everybody from your past because of where you
are today and where you will be tomorrow. 358
Take the opportunity today to do The Work. 359
Take the opportunity today to be present and engaged. 360
Take the opportunity today to really look to see if you're recycling everything you
possibly can. 361
Take the opportunity today to play a game. 362
Take the opportunity today to shop in a local store. 363
Take the opportunity today to visit an awe inspiring building. 364
Take the opportunity today to NOT watch TV. At all! 365

17354781R00230

Printed in Great Britain
by Amazon